WARD LOCK'S

FIRST PICTURE

ENCYCLOPEDIA

Written and illustrated by Herbert Pothorn

WARD LOCK LIMITED · LONDON

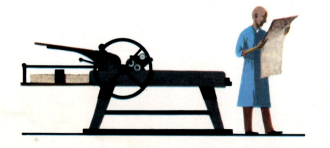

© Ward Lock London 1974
Illustrations © Droemersche Verlaganstalt Th. Knaur
Nachf. München/Zürich
ISBN 0 7063 1652 5
This edition published in Great Britain in 1974 by
Ward Lock Limited, 116 Baker Street, London
W1M 2BB

Filmset in Century by Yendall & Co, London
Printed in Spain by H. Fournier, S.A., Vitoria

CONTENTS

PLANTS

THROUGH THE AGES

THE EARTH

THE SKY

GAMES AND SPORTS

About three hundred years ago there lived a man who was born in Bohemia and whose name was Jan Amos Komensky. He was a very learned man and like other learned men at that time he changed his name into Latin and called himself Comenius.

When Comenius was sixty years old he published a book to which he gave the Latin title *Orbis pictus*. It showed the world in pictures and was the very first picture book for children—and for a long time the only one.

But later on thousands of children's books were published in all parts of the world and again and again people tried to write a book which would describe everything that was in the world and explain all that was known.

A book which tries to do this is called an encyclopaedia, but in actual fact there has never been any such book. If anyone tried to describe every single thing that is in the world his book would have to be hundreds of thousands of pages long and even then the descriptions would have to be so short and the illustrations so tiny that you would not be able to see the pictures or understand the explanations.

But if, on the other hand, the pictures were large and clear and everything were described in full detail, there would not be room in any book for all of it. Perhaps it would not matter so very much if some things were left out, but it is not always easy to know what to leave out. It is, however, always very important to put in the things we like most. In this book, for instance, which is a little like an encyclopaedia, you will find a picture of a zebra, but you won't find a picture of a machine gun, not even a very small one. Don't imagine that the man who wrote this book thinks that zebras are more important than machine guns. He has left the machine gun out simply because he doesn't like machine guns as much as he likes zebras.

You may very likely open this book and see a picture of something you already know quite well. Then you will probably say, "I know all this already!" But look at the picture more closely and you will find a lot of things are different from those you know, for many of the pictures in this book show things from other lands.

See how many differences you can discover, for it is interesting to find out how other people make everyday things—and how often they are really very much the same thing in the end. Now go on turning the pages; you will come across many things that you have never even heard of. And if you are so clever that you already know exactly what an olive tree looks like you must remember that there are many other children who do not even know the name because they live in countries where there aren't any olive trees and because they have never travelled to the places where these trees grow. The same is true about many other things, animals, plants, scenery, blocks of flats and underground railways.

Some children live in cities and go to school each day by bus or underground train, but there are other children who live in the country and who have never seen the underground. These country children know far more about the fields and woods than town children: if they pick up a tiny blue feather, for instance, they know without troubling to think that it must have been dropped by a jay.

Of all the thousands of varieties of birds in the world only a few are described in this book. And the same is true of many other things, such as trees, fish, cars or Red Indian tribes. For a book such as this can only include a few examples from each kind of thing. If you are specially interested in anything you will easily be able to find other books about it.

The book is not arranged alphabetically so you can't use it as though it were a dictionary where Artillery follows directly after Artichoke. You will not find Zebra at the end, but on the page about Africa.

The book begins with what you all know, with houses and streets like those you live in, and it ends with what is very far away, with Uranus and Neptune. So you pass from what you know best to what you know least, from what is close at hand to what is most distant, and on the journey from one to the other you will find out something about your world and what happens in it.

If you should be in a hurry you will find an index at the end where everything in the book from Ants to Zoo is alphabetically listed. But don't be in too much of a hurry.

HOUSES AND TOWNS

AT HOME

The first thing a child gets to know in the world is his home, the house where he lives with his father and mother, brothers and sisters. The house may only have very few rooms or, if the family is large, it may perhaps have a large number of rooms.

People have not always lived in houses and there are still places where home is not a house. In certain countries far from here there live children whose home is a forest or a field. The walls of the room are nothing but bushes or interwoven twigs and the roof is made of branches covered with a few big leaves. You will be hearing more about these children later on.

We live in houses and the houses are either built in terraces along the streets or they stand in gardens with walls or hedges round them. There are many different kinds of building, some so small that there is only just enough room for one family inside and others so big that they contain many homes side by side and one on top of another. These often have balconies which take the place of a garden, for so many families live in the big cities that there is not enough room for everyone to have a garden.

Most children live at home with their parents until they are grown up. When they have learnt a profession or when they want to get married they generally go and live in a flat or a house of their own.

Grab   Crane   Bulldozer   Tractor

BUILDING A HOUSE

The bricklayer puts one brick on top of another, holding them together with mortar, which is a mixture of lime, sand and water, and in a few weeks the house begins to take shape. The work is often completed much faster than you would believe possible. This is especially so when cranes are used. It is only since cranes were invented that men have been able to build quickly the tall blocks of flats which have sprung up in all the larger towns during the past few years. Cranes are not used, however, for small houses such as you can see being built on the right. All that is necessary is a simple scaffolding with ladders, planks and poles.

On top of the block of flats in the background you can see a little tree with ribbons tied to it. It used to be the custom everywhere to put up a tree decorated with ribbons or to hoist a flag as soon as a house had reached roof height. And then the owner, the architect, the builder, and the workmen would hold a celebration. This is still sometimes done in parts of Germany and Austria. All the people who have had anything to do with the building gather together. The architect makes a speech congratulating all the men for working so hard. Then the whole party goes to an inn where the owner orders a barrel of beer and a splendid supper.

WHO LIVES HERE?

Very often you only have to look at a house to tell what kind of people own it.

You can see at once that Number 13 was once a very fine house, but that must have been quite a long time ago. The inside is very likely as shabby as the outside. The owner really should do something about it. After all, the people who live in the house all pay rent and the owner could spend part of the money on keeping his property in order. But perhaps he is an old skinflint.

Number 15 is a good example of a well kept old house. Two ladies inherited it and they try to keep it in perfect order for they know that the better a house is cared for the more it is worth; they also want everything to be in good condition so that the younger relatives, to whom they intend to leave the house, will enjoy living in it.

An elderly gentleman and his housekeeper live at Number 17. This is a very quiet house, a little old fashioned, perhaps, but very cosy.

The old gentleman is probably a naturalist or something of the sort. His windows are often lit up late at night which means that he is working, perhaps writing a book about butterflies and beetles. You can see some modern flats behind Number 17. The first floor of this block has been rented by a dentist. The second floor is occupied by the flat and offices of a solicitor. Above him there lives a tradesman who is making a lot of money. Before very long he will be made a director; then he will buy a house of his own.

Number 19 looks like the home of a magician and I expect a magician did live there once. Today it is inhabited by a radio fanatic, a very odd fellow who says he knows how to make aerials out of old umbrella frames. Number 21 used to be stables. Hardly any horses are left in the town today so the man to whom the stables belonged turned them into a house. The people who live there are very glad to have a home of their own at last.

IN TOWN

This picture shows you what many of the smaller towns in continental Europe look like. This is the kind of street and market place you will see when you go abroad. The church with the twin towers is very different from most of the churches you see in England. It is a little like St. Paul's and was built at about the same time, more than two hundred years ago. You will be able to read all about it in the guide book which will tell you the name of the saint to whom it is dedicated. The church behind the tall, steep-roofed houses must be twice as old as the church in the market place. It is a Gothic church and will of course be mentioned in the guide book too. The street on the right leads up to the palace. A prince lived there once, but it is now a library and Art Gallery.

Power Station   Gasworks

One day the baker did not feel like baking any bread. He decided to go for a walk instead. On the way he felt very hungry so he went to the butcher and asked for some sausages. "You can't buy any sausages today," said the butcher, "I was too upset to

Bread and Cakes

Meat and sausages

Eggs, milk, butter and cheese

Fruit and vegetables

Crockery

Shoes   Clothes

Furniture

18

WHAT THE TOWN NEEDS

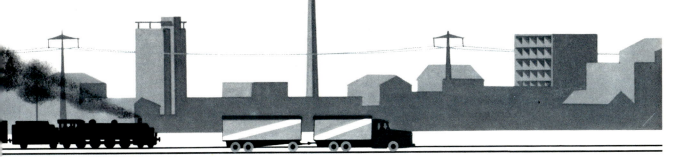

Slaughter house and Cold storage   Television mast   Warehouses

make any this morning because there was no bread for breakfast." The baker thought he would have his hair cut. "I can't do it," said the hairdresser, "I'm too weak; I couldn't get any bread for breakfast." So the baker hurried back to his bakery as fast as he could. Everyone depends on other people!

Supermarket

Chemist

Hairdresser

Electrician

Books

Stationery

Toys

Flowers

Pram · Scooter · Tricycle · Bicycle · Moped

EVERYTHING ON WHEELS

If we had nothing on wheels it would take us much longer to get from one place to another. If there were no prams, for instance, babies would have to be carried along the streets or into the park until they had learnt to walk. And children who had no scooters would take twice as long to get from home to the playground and back again.

When a boy is old enough his father often gives him a bicycle or he may buy one with his own money. At first he is extremely proud but it is not long before he is bored with it. He feels he simply must have a moped. The moped makes a shattering noise but that is exactly why the boy likes it so much. All the same a moped is not as good as a motor cycle and so quite soon the boy longs for a motor cycle. This is a very noisy machine too, but the sound of the motor cycle is not quite so strident as that of the moped, it is a deep, muffled, satisfying and

almost solemn roar, especially when the machine is really heavy.

After the motor cycles come the little two seaters, trim little metal boxes on four wheels that were often made before their owners were born. And these are followed by full-sized cars, small, large, expensive, fast or slow, cars of every conceivable colour, gay and shining like Easter eggs, cars in which there is room not only for the whole family but for bags, suitcases, tents and lilos; and fast, streamlined sports cars in which there is only just room for one small bag and two people whose legs are not particularly long.

Sometimes you may still find an old horse-drawn carriage on the road amongst all the cars. It is always fun to take a ride in a horse-drawn carriage especially if it happens to be your birthday or someone's wedding or even if it is just a very fine day.

Station wagon

Small saloon

20

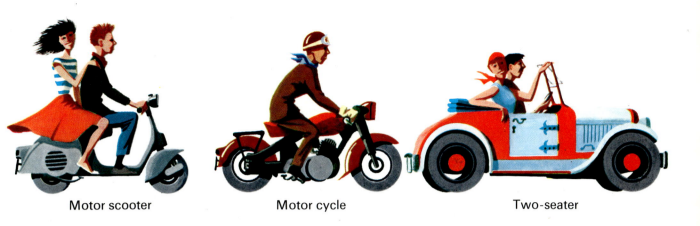

Motor scooter   Motor cycle   Two-seater

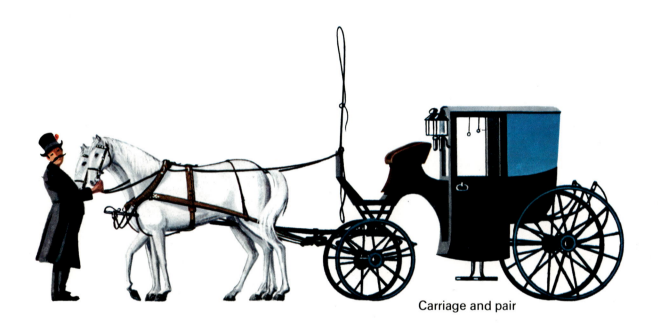

Carriage and pair

Large convertible

Sports car

CONTROLLING THE TRAFFIC

There are traffic lights and road signs at almost every street corner. All have a special meaning and serve a useful purpose, even though you may think some of them unnecessary.

It is not at all difficult to understand most road signs as they are almost the same everywhere in Europe, but a driver must always be on the alert in busy streets, so as not to miss any of them. People ought not to drive if they are tired or ill or have been drinking, even if they think they will be all right.

Careless driving can lead to a damaged car, a permanent injury, or even imprisonment. Worst of all it could kill someone.

On the page opposite you can see a busy crossing in a large town in Germany, with tram and bus stops and an underground station. Can you see the drain?

There are underground railways in London, Glasgow, Paris, Berlin, Hamburg, Moscow, Rome, Naples, Budapest, New York and Tokyo, and one is being built in Amsterdam.

SIGNS GIVING ORDERS (circular)

Maximum speed 70 mph

Stop and give way

Give way to traffic on major road

No waiting

No stopping (Clearway)

School crossing patrol

No cycling or moped riding

Give priority to vehicles from opposite direction

Buses and coaches prohibited

No pedestrians

Turn left ahead

Keep left

Pass either side

Route for cyclists and moped riders (compulsory)

WARNING SIGNS (triangular)

Crossroads

Bend to right

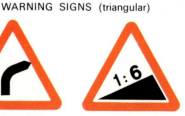
Steep hill upwards

Pedestrian crossing

Road works

Slippery road

Level crossing without barrier

Wild animals

Horses or ponies

Low flying aircraft

THE FIRE SERVICE

The danger of fire in towns is far less acute than it used to be, because houses are hardly ever built of wood as they once were and there are fewer open fires. All the same it is necessary to be on the alert because there are many other ways in which a fire may be started today. A faulty electric cable may cause one, and so may a gas leak. In nearly every street you will find a fire alarm or a telephone box from which it is possible to give the alarm in a few seconds and tell the fire service exactly where the fire has broken out. The most important thing in dealing with fire is not to waste a single minute: the fire must not be allowed to spread.

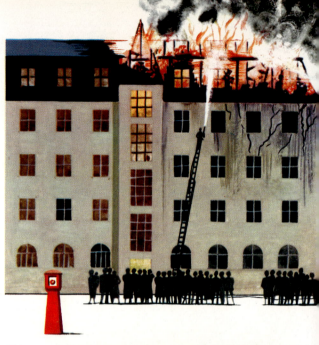

THE AMBULANCE AND POLICE SERVICE

Telephones also serve to sound the alarm in case of accident. The police and the ambulance service can be summoned instantly either from a special police telephone or from the nearest public call box. Then with bell ringing or klaxon shrieking the ambulance rushes to the scene of the accident. The ambulance men and doctor give first aid to anyone who is injured or take him straight to hospital, while the policeman finds out how it all happened, questions the witnesses and writes a report.

THE HOSPITAL

All over the world there are too few hospitals to meet the needs of the people. New hospitals are being built everywhere. Even the healthiest person may one day have to go into hospital. There is no need to be frightened or nervous, for you will be looked after and cared for and the sooner you have the proper treatment, the sooner you will get better. Altogether there are hundreds of different illnesses and only a small proportion of the causes of these are known. We have to find the cause of an illness before we can cure it and hospital laboratories help to do this.

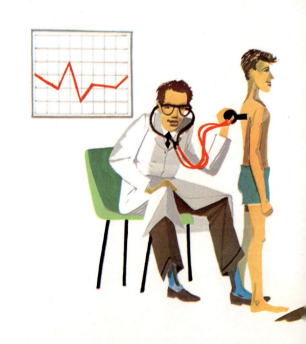

WORKMEN

Locksmith

Joiner

House painter

Tailor

Milliner

Cobbler

Upholsterer

Fitter

Motor mechanic

Clockmaker

ARTISTS

Sculptor   Painter   Writer   Composer

Actor   Singer   Dancers   Musician

CRAFTSMEN

Embroidress   Metal worker   Potter

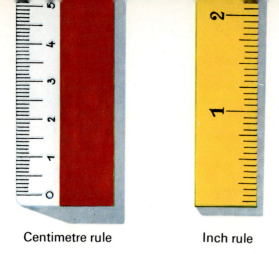

Centimetre rule   Inch rule

WEIGHING AND MEASURING

Without weights and measures you would not be able to find out how much you had grown in the past year. The transport manager would not know how great a load a lorry could take without breaking down. A few of the more important instruments for weighing and measuring are shown here.

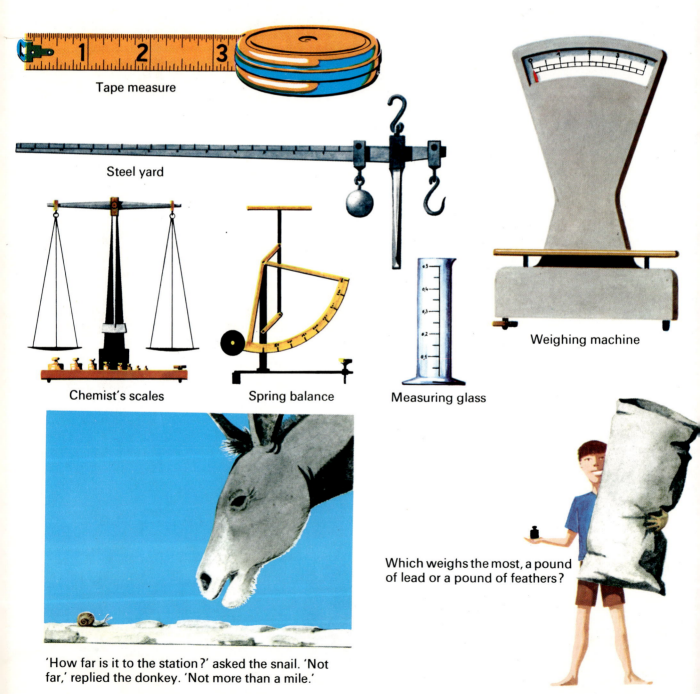

Tape measure

Steel yard

Weighing machine

Chemist's scales   Spring balance   Measuring glass

Which weighs the most, a pound of lead or a pound of feathers?

'How far is it to the station?' asked the snail. 'Not far,' replied the donkey. 'Not more than a mile.'

TIME

The clock ticks once in every second and 60 times in every minute. In one hour it ticks 3,600 times and in one day it ticks 86,400 times. In one year it ticks 31,536,000 times. What are you doing during all that time? You spend 100 days sleeping and 100 days working; the rest of the time you can do as you like.

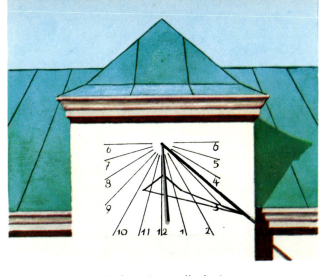

A sundial on the wall of a house

HOW FAST ARE THEY?

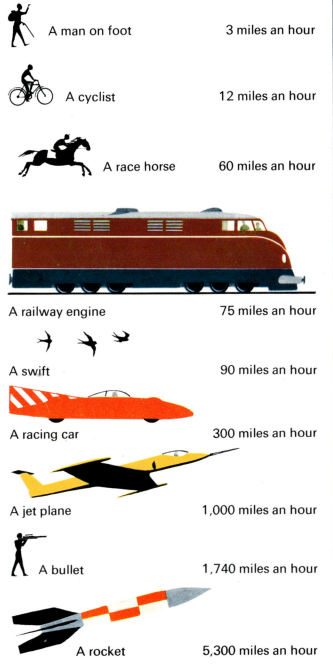

A man on foot	3 miles an hour
A cyclist	12 miles an hour
A race horse	60 miles an hour
A railway engine	75 miles an hour
A swift	90 miles an hour
A racing car	300 miles an hour
A jet plane	1,000 miles an hour
A bullet	1,740 miles an hour
A rocket	5,300 miles an hour

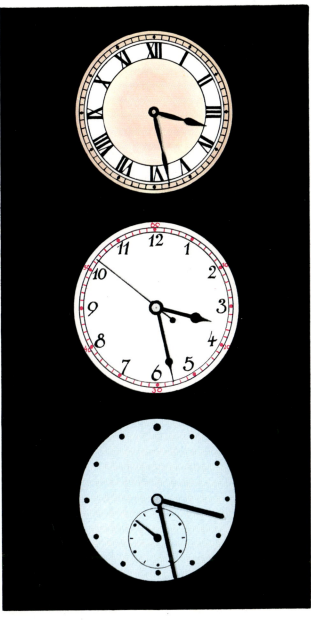

Top: A clock face with Roman numerals. Centre: A clock face showing the 24 hours, with a seconds hand. Below: A dial without numerals.

VIA AIR MAIL
MIT LUFTPOST
PAR AVION

BY AIR MA
PAR AVIO
हवाई डाक

Aircraft and mail boat for letters and parcels going overseas

Mail van on the railway

Post office bus, small van for collecting letters, large van for parcels

Durch Eilboten
Exprès

R 492 a 3 Z
München 23

Postman and express messenger

THE POST OFFICE

There is no end to the things the post office does for us. First of all it ensures that our letters, parcels and telegrams are delivered. It also provides us with letter boxes, telephone boxes and stamp machines. In some countries the post office even runs a bus service. The bus shown here is yellow and the letter box, stamp machine, telephone box and mail van are all yellow too. In England the post office collects the money for our wireless and television licences and pensions are paid through the post office. With its help we can send money to each other and if you want to save money you can open a post office savings account.

Governments are always having new stamps printed and this is particularly important for stamp collectors. A stamp that is no longer in current use is worth more than one which is still valid and its value goes on increasing with time. It is possible to pay hundreds of pounds for certain stamps.

PRIMARY AND SECONDARY SCHOOL

Sometimes when you aren't getting on too well and lessons seem specially difficult, you can't help wishing you were still at the primary school. Nobody there made you sit still for hours on end and nobody kept telling you to pay attention and keep your eyes on your book. You did nothing but play the whole morning long, you built houses with your toy bricks, you drew with crayons, you cut out little men and did all sorts of delightful things. No one minded if you were late once or twice.

Secondary school is a very different, very serious matter indeed. You must always be punctual. The teacher makes you sit quite still and listen carefully when he is explaining something. And then you have to spend most of the evening doing homework. And this goes on day after day, week after week, year after year. Most children have to go to school for at least ten years, others for much longer.

But at the end of every school year there are the long summer holidays. On the last day of term the school reports are given out or sent to your parents and you wonder whether yours will be good or bad.

THE LIBRARY

Public libraries contain books dealing with every branch of knowledge. Anyone may go there and borrow books about the subject which interests him most or about which he must know for his studies. He may also borrow novels and stories.

In the great libraries of the world are pre-served not only printed books but old manu-scripts which are of special importance.

In most towns there are special libraries for children. They look much the same as other libraries except that the shelves are lower and the chairs and tables are smaller. Often there are games and story-readings in children's libraries.

THE ZOO

A walk through the Zoo is like visiting different and distant parts of the globe. In a single afternoon you can get some idea of America, Asia, Africa and Australia and you can find out about animals which you would otherwise only be able to see after long journeys.

Most zoos are in or near large towns, and nowadays there are also big safari and wild animal parks in most countries, where people can see and study the animals in natural surroundings.

THE MUSEUM

A museum is a collection of works of art and curious or interesting objects. Every country possesses museums for all branches of the arts and sciences. On the left you see a room in a natural history museum. The large animal is a reconstruction of a tyrannosaurus, a giant lizard of prehistoric times. Animals like this lived on earth 100 million years ago. On the right are two rooms in a museum of ancient pots and sculpture.

THE CIRCUS

In the days when there were no cinemas, no radio and no television, there was great excitement when the circus arrived in the town, but nowadays nobody seems to get very excited about it any more. Yet it is just as fascinating as it ever was. Circus people form a very close community, travelling together in their own caravans from town to town. In spite of some changes the circus is really just the same as it always was.

35

THE THEATRE AND CINEMA

You will know what a cinema looks like so there is no need to describe it. But the theatre is quite a different matter. It is so full of interest that the picture of it must take up a whole page. This picture has been specially chosen to show you what the stage looks like, not on the evening of the performance, but during a rehearsal.

Two actors are rehearsing their dialogue. In the front of the picture, with his back towards you, stands the producer who is directing the play. The young woman sitting near him is his assistant. She is writing down in a notebook all that the producer says. The scenery (which includes the wings and all the objects needed for the setting) is only partly erected, just enough for the actors to see how much room they have.

The whole stage with its lighting fixtures is very high, far higher than it appears from the auditorium. This is necessary because when the scene is changed the wings and backcloth have to be raised right up out of sight of the audience.

In the front of the picture to the right you will notice an opening in the floor with steps going down. Through this objects which are needed for the set can be quickly brought up or removed from sight. The opening is also useful if an actor has to look as if he were just coming up from the cellar or rising from his grave.

The division between the actual stage and the orchestra is called the footlights because it is occupied by a number of lamps, some of them coloured, by means of which the actors can be properly lit. In the centre of the footlights you will see the prompter's box. The prompter sits inside there all through the performance, with the book of the play in front of him, ready to whisper the words in case one of the actors forgets his part.

To the left and right of the prompter's box there are openings in the stage floor which enable the man who is in charge of the lighting effects to see onto the boards. He controls the lighting to fit in with the action of the play and the producer's instructions.

On the evening of the performance the public should not be able to see anything that goes on behind the stage. After all the rehearsals everything should go without a hitch. But of course sometimes there is one. On one occasion the hero had to point his revolver at the villain crying: "Die then, traitor!" as the shot rang through the theatre. But the revolver just wouldn't go off. All the villain could do was to clutch wildly at his breast, shout out "Bang!" and fall down dead.

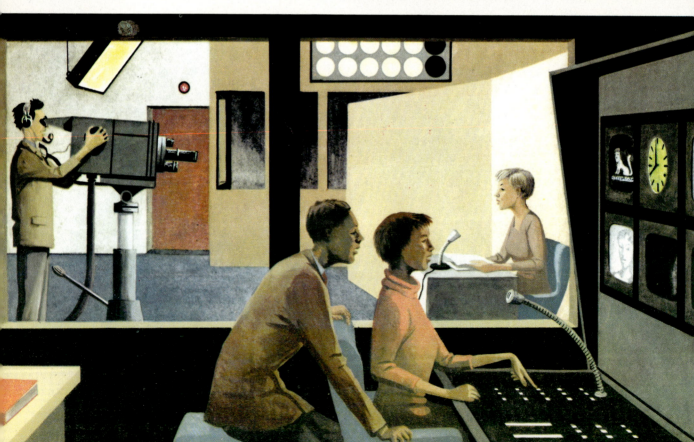

FILMS AND TELEVISION

Since the invention of films and television people hardly ever spend an evening telling stories as they once did. As soon as they have finished their work they either go to the cinema or sit down in front of the television. Even if you only go occasionally to the cinemas and only look at television now and then you can't help realising what remarkable inventions these are.

Film actors and producers go about their business in an entirely different way from those who work only for the stage. When a film is made the scenes do not follow one another in the direct sequence which you see when you go to the cinema. Suppose, for instance, that a certain room appears several times in the course of a film. That room is constructed in the studio and all the scenes that take place in it are filmed one after another. Then if the producer is satisfied the room is dismantled.

At the top of the opposite page you will see a small film studio. The photographers have brought their camera in close to the man who is reading the news bulletin, so that the viewers can see his face. The microphone is over the camera and the studio lights are on.

The lower picture shows a television studio. The producer and the picture controller are sitting at the control desk, which consists of a table on which there are a number of switches and buttons and a wall in which small television screens show everything that the cameras take. It is the picture controller's job to connect the various cameras in the right order. When as you see here, something is just about to be televised she first of all puts through the signal for that particular station, then she switches over to the camera which is focussing on the announcer. As soon as the announcer has finished speaking she switches over to a camera in another studio where perhaps a television play is being acted or she connects with a mobile camera outside where some important event may be taking place.

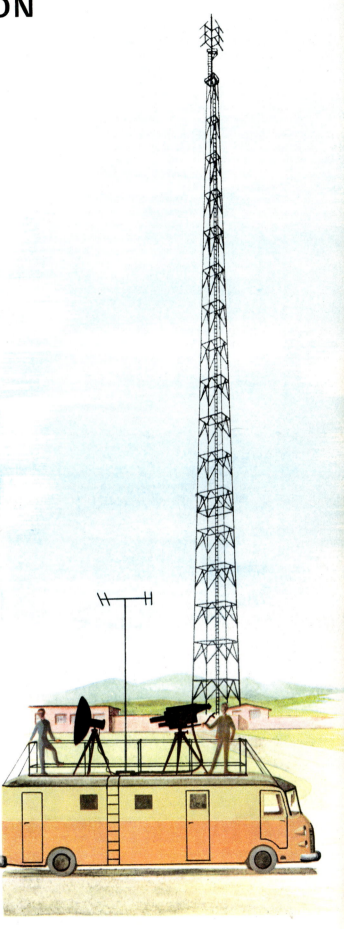

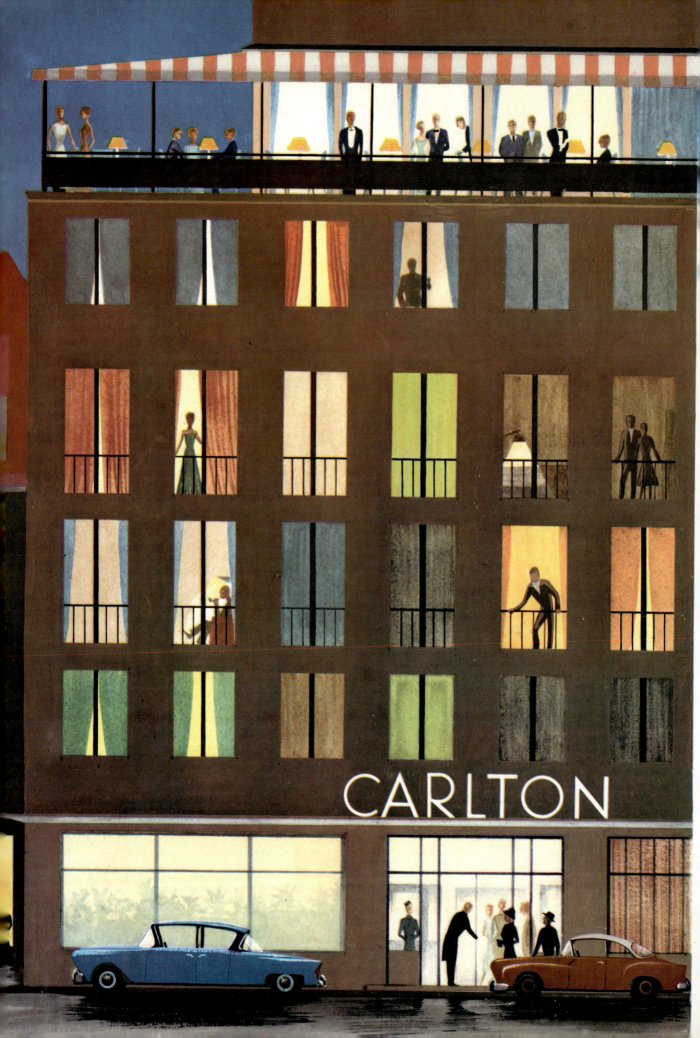

HOTELS

Hotel names tell you a lot about what the hotels are like, or what they want to sound like. If a hotel is called The Carlton it sounds expensive and exclusive. Any hotel called The Grand or The Imperial surely must be large and luxurious. As for The Royal, it must be fit for Kings and Queens. A large number of hotels are called after famous people such as Wellington, Nelson, Queen Victoria, the Duke of York or the Prince of Wales, but that is not to say that any of these celebrities have ever really stayed there.

The most interesting names belong to some of the older hotels which were once coaching inns. Among these are the Swan, the White Hart, the Bull, the Bell, the Crown, the White Horse, the Red Lion, the Feathers and the Boar. Many of these names were taken from the heraldic shield of the reigning king or lord of the manor at the time when the inn was built. The white horse was the badge of the house of Hanover, the boar was the badge of Richard III, the white hart the emblem of Richard II and the feathers that of the Black Prince.

When you are travelling you do not only go to a hotel to sleep but also to enjoy all the comforts of good food and drink and pleasant surroundings. The manager, the head porter and probably the head waiter can all speak several languages so that guests who come from foreign countries can always make themselves understood.

There is a large staff to look after the guests, chambermaids, pageboys, waiters, the wine waiter, the housekeeper and the chef. It is fun to watch how busy they all are and how they give the impression that they have far too much to do. Sometimes during the summer months when guests are continually coming and going there is indeed a great deal going on. At other times of the year it is often very slack in the hotel unless a millionaire should suddenly arrive who expects everyone to be at his beck and call. Then there is a tremendous commotion. The pageboys and chambermaids scurry to and fro, the waiters carry in the dishes as fast as they can and the commissionaire keeps saying "Yes, sir!" and "Oui, Madame!" and "Buona sera!" and "Auf Wiedersehen!"

FACTORIES

At one time all tools such as files, for instance, were made by hand. Now they are made in factories. It is not so very long since brushes were all made by hand, but now there are special factories for making them. The many small, often insignificant, workshops of former times, places where wire was drawn and nails were made, the old glass works, soap works, paper and woollen mills have all grown into gigantic industries, for there is a far greater demand for all these and many other things than ever before and it would be impossible for the small workshops to produce them in sufficient quantity.

Many of the things we need today, things like bicycles, railway engines and cars could not be made at all if there were no factories. It would be far too expensive and would take much too long to produce such things in small workshops. When a new cycle or car model is to be put on the market the engineers spend a long time thinking about it, making calculations and experiments and only when the model has been split up into its smallest components can it go into production.

An arrangement such as you see above in a car factory is known as a conveyor belt

because it passes the work on from one man to the next. Each workman does only the one special task allotted to him. Two men are here shown assembling the engine, the next are installing the radiator. Then comes the steering wheel, the petrol tank, the brakes and finally the body, the wheels and the upholstery. Thousands of hands are working on the job and the car is completed in a matter of minutes.

It may seem very boring to work in a car factory and do the same thing day after day, never to do anything but tighten a screw or put in a rivet from eight o'clock in the morning until five in the afternoon. But the workmen don't find it at all boring. They must be continually on the alert not to make a mistake and to finish each process dead on time so that the next man is not kept waiting. And the longer a man has been doing one particular job the more skilled he becomes and the less likely he is to make a mistake.

It is often said that the article produced by the old workshops were well made whereas factory goods are slipshod. But this is not true. Some workshops produced excellent goods while others were unreliable and in the same way some factories turn out better

articles than others. It all depends on the people who are doing the work and no one should imagine that all factory work is mechanical and automatic. There are many process of which a machine is incapable and if the workmen and the foreman were not constantly on the look out for faults, some very rickety cars would be put on the road.

THE PRINTING PRESS

When printing was just beginning, a separate piece of wood had to be carved out for each letter. Then a new method was invented, using moulds to make moveable metal letters. Still later, machines could make whole lines of words on one strip of metal.

In each case the letters or lines were made into complete pages, locked up into frames

and inked. The paper was then rolled over the inked pages. Nowadays other methods, using photographic reproduction, are used.

Steam engine

Luggage van

Diesel passenger train

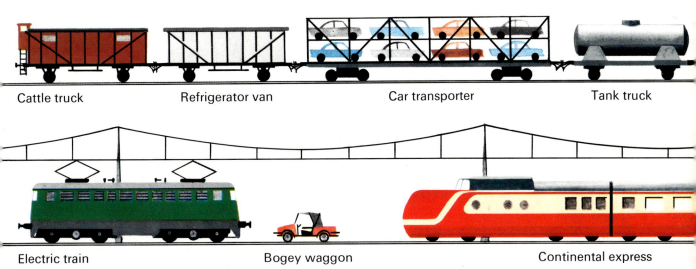

Cattle truck

Refrigerator van

Car transporter

Tank truck

Electric train

Bogey waggon

Continental express

THE RAILWAYS

A great many people used not to like railway stations because of the smell which was peculiar to railways. Other people liked the smell because it reminded them of holidays, of journeys to distant places. Such people sometimes went to the station just for the pure pleasure of it even when they had no train to catch.

Trains are not so dirty as they used to be and they do not smell as much, for the old steam engines which belched smoke and smut as they chugged along have given way to Diesel and electric trains. The picture on the left shows a German station as it looks to the train driver when he is approaching it. The points in the foreground have been shifted so that he can go straight ahead. The white rectangle, which he could see some way

back, told him that it was safe to drive into the station. If the points had been shifted a white diagonal would have shown instead.

The points are regulated from the signal box which you can see immediately behind the buffers at the end of one pair of lines. Buffers are placed at the end of every line and are always marked with a red sign so that they are visible from a distance. Not only the points but also the signals are worked from the signal box. There are well over a hundred different kinds of signals; boards and poles supplied with pulleys and moveable arms containing green, red and yellow lights. They are more difficult to understand than road traffic signs. One or two of them have been included here and there in these pages.

Boeing 747 Jumbo jet

Opposite: The supersonic aircraft
Concorde and a helicopter

THE AIRPORT

People who are so unfortunate as to live near an airport have great and increasing cause for complaint. They can never sleep undisturbed and even during the day the noise of planes taking off is so deafening that it is quite impossible to concentrate.

It is essential that engineers should invent a means of muffling the roar of jets. They have already begun to do so but there is still a lot to be done before the noise is low enough.

If you are in a great hurry, however, you are delighted when you hear the ear-splitting sound of the mighty engines starting up. "What a powerful machine," you say to yourself, "I shall be there in no time." Then you look at the timetable and say, "Now if I were going from London to New York by boat and train I shouldn't arrive till next week. With the jet I shall be there in a few hours." New supersonic planes may eventually make travel even quicker.

Planes are getting larger and faster all the time and the runways are growing longer and longer. In the early days of aeroplanes the machine could take off from a small field. Now every airport must have a concrete runway at least 50 yards wide and 2 miles long. It is built in the direction of the prevailing wind because it is easier for planes to land and take off in the face of the wind. At night there is a row of lights on either side of the runway. Every airport is controlled from a tower in which there are officials in charge of all taking-off and landing operations. They contact the pilots by radio some time before the great planes are approaching the airport. It may happen that the runway is not free: another plane may be about to take off. In this case the machine which is coming down must wait, circling round until the signal comes through from the control tower that the runway is clear and it is safe to land.

Helicopters, which are slower and much smaller, can take off and land without a concrete runway. If necessary they can take straight off in an almost vertical line from any field or sportsground providing it is fairly level.

ROADS AND BRIDGES

Nearly every road that leads across country from town to town has to find its way over valleys, deep cuttings, rivers or railway lines. It is only with the help of bridges that these obstacles can be overcome, bridges of every variety, many of them remarkable works of architecture and engineering. The simplest bridges are constructed of wood but their span is limited and they cannot bear much weight. Bridges of stone, iron or concrete have far greater possibilities. Bridges of vast span like the one shown at the top of the page are always constructed mainly of iron and steel. Such bridges are called suspension bridges because the track is suspended from steel ropes which in turn are supported by tall stanchions. The longer the bridge the taller the stanchions.

The lower picture shows a bridge of steel girders being built. The steel plates are being riveted together piece by piece and the crane makes it possible to do this with the minimum use of scaffolding. In a bridge of this kind the supports must be placed closer together than with the suspension bridge.

When the bridge has been completed there is often a formal opening. A ribbon is stretched from one side of the bridge to the other and a titled lady, a minister or perhaps the mayor makes a short speech, cuts the ribbon and is the first to walk or drive over the bridge.

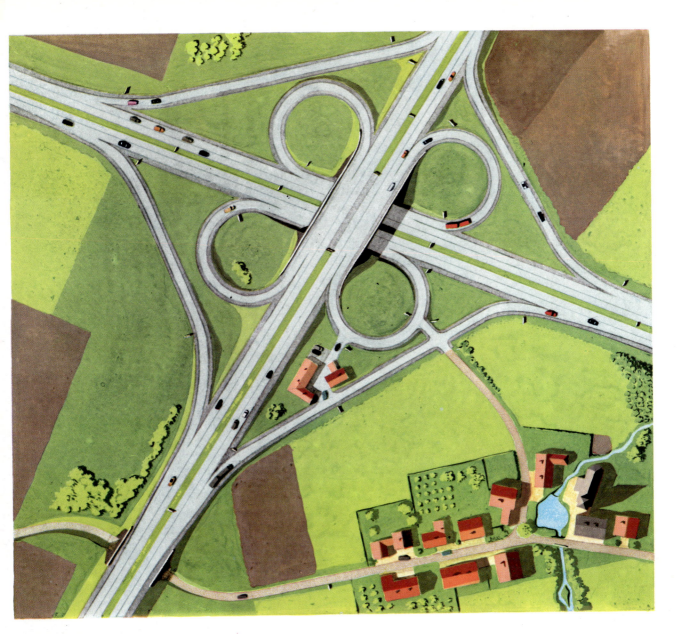

MOTORWAYS

Some of the farmers who live near the cloverleaf crossing in this picture have had to give up part of their land. They were not pleased about this at first, but they have been paid for it, and now they are much happier close to a great highway instead of being shut off in the depths of the country. Once they have reached the crossing they can motor in any direction far more quickly and conveniently than when they had to travel along the winding country roads of earlier days. There are no roads branching to left and right of the motor highways, so no car ever has to cross in front of another. Where traffic is dense this is a great advantage because it is usually at crossroads that accidents occur.

Until recently the old country roads were enough for the traffic that passed along them. There were not so many cars then and there was no fast driving. Today it is impossible to imagine a country without motor roads.

The picture shows, as if from the air, how one road passes beneath another by means of a bridge and how the loops of the clover crossing enable drivers to change direction without interfering with other motorists who wish to go straight ahead. When you look at these roads, which are in America, remember that the traffic drives on the right hand side. The buildings which stand by the loop which is nearest to the village are a filling station and a restaurant.

MINING

Miners are very much like the dwarfs in fairy tales who dig for gold and precious stones in the bowels of the earth, except that the miners are looking not only for jewels and precious metals but also for coal, salt, limestone, quartz and slate, all of which are very important to men and would be of no interest at all to dwarfs.

Dwarfs work only with pick axes and shovels but miners use tools which are far more complicated, pneumatic drills, electric hoists and blasting apparatus, all of which make their laborious work easier. The picture on the opposite page shows a cross section of a mine. The broad black stripes in the earth represent the coal seams. In order to get at them a deep shaft is sunk and from this shaft horizontal galleries are cut.

Above the shaft opening stands the pit head, a tall tower with wire ropes running round a wheel. This is for lowering the cage and drawing it up to the surface. The cage comes up full of coal and tips its contents into the small railway trucks. Similar trucks convey the coal along the underground galleries, but they are smaller in size because the passage is often very narrow. The trucks can be moved to other, higher or lower, galleries by means of hoists.

This is what is happening in the lefthand shaft, which is known as a blind shaft because it does not go right up to the surface. It enables the trucks to be brought from different levels to the gallery from which the coal can be pushed down an incline into the cage.

DAMS

In the winter and spring, rain from the hills often swells the rivers until they overflow their banks and flood the roads and countryside. It is to prevent the danger of floods that dams have been constructed in many river valleys. A dam is a high wall of stone and concrete which forces the water to form an artificial lake. In the drier seasons of the year the water can be slowly released once more.

As it rushes out it can be made to do important work. It passes through turbines, which are rather like watermills only much more powerful. These turbines generate electric power which can be used to drive machines or give light to houses and factories in the district. The picture gives a bird's eye view of the dam; it is the same sort of view as that of the clover crossing on page 49.

THE HARBOUR

If you like going to the station to watch the trains you will almost certainly enjoy a walk by the harbour. There are many things to see. If you are lucky you may find someone to show you round. He will tell you about the things you can see.

"That vessel over there," he says, "is off to South America with 500 passengers aboard. That building you see over there is the customs house, where passengers have to show their passports when they go on board or come ashore. The wall by which the ship is moored is called the quay. Those things the ships are tied to are called bollards. The structure over there is called a pier. The wooden piles at the end are to prevent boats from running into the end of the pier. It wouldn't hurt the pier but the boat would probably be damaged. That small boat hurrying across the harbour is a tug. Its job is to tow the big ships to their berths. You will notice that there are sacks filled with cork and rope, fenders as they are

called, all round the sides and front of the tug. These act as shock absorbers and prevent friction against the harbour walls and the sides of other ships.

"That vessel over there is a merchant ship. It is alongside the quay where the warehouses and cranes are. In the distance out there you can make out a lighthouse. It is fitted with a revolving light that sweeps across the water far and wide after dark. The dam on which it is built is called a mole. Lighthouses are often built also on rocks or sandbanks and there are lightbuoys and lightships too that send out warnings from the open sea."

If you visit a harbour you might see piles of timber, waggons of coal, bales of wood-pulp, sacks of grain, cars and machinery, and many other cargoes. Some of these things will have arrived from other countries. Some of them will be going to other countries, for trading goes on between all nations of the world.

THE CHANNEL TUNNEL

Almost 200 years ago someone suggested that a tunnel should be dug beneath the English Channel but it is still unbuilt.

One reason for the delay has been the objections of military leaders. They feared that a tunnel connecting Britain with the continent of Europe might be used by invading armies in time of war.

A few years ago they decided to think again about building a Channel tunnel. A special study group was set up to examine the problem. The group studied different methods of travel between Britain and the rest of Europe. Some people thought that bigger and better car ferries should be built. Some suggested that a huge bridge should span the Channel. Others thought that a floating bridge might be better. After study-

ing all these ideas, the group decided that the best way would be to build a tunnel underneath the sea. They surveyed the sea-bed to find the best route for the tunnel to take. The surveys showed that a layer of chalk lay under the sea-bed. Chalk is easy to tunnel through and does not let in water. The team recommended that a high-speed two-way rail tunnel should be built. Cars and lorries would be loaded onto long flat trucks and carried through the tunnel. A special rail link would be built to connect London with the tunnel entrance.

All these proposals were discussed in Parliament in 1973. If it goes ahead, it is planned to connect Folkestone in England to Calais in France, a distance of 32 miles—23 miles under the sea. There will be two main tunnels, each carrying a single railway track. These will be linked by a number of crossovers and a service tunnel. When the tunnel is completed we will be able to travel very quickly to continental cities.

THE COUNTRY

THE VILLAGE

If you compare village life with town life you will soon realise that it is not true to say that a village is a miniature town. Everything is quite different, the houses, the streets, even the air you breathe. The houses in the village street often stand cheek by jowl as in a town street, but they are seldom more than two storeys high, though some have attics. Nearly all have gardens at the back, while the smallest space in front is full of flowers.

There may be one or two modern houses but most of the cottages and houses are old, some as much as four hundred years old, and they are built of stone, flint or timber and plaster, whichever materials lay closest to hand in that particular district. Many of the cottages are thatched.

The most important buildings in the village are the church, the rectory, the school, the inn and the house which once belonged to the squire. There are usually several shops, the butcher's, the grocer's and the village stores crammed with every kind of article. The village is surrounded by the open country dotted with farmhouses.

Some villages are so small that there is no school and the children have to go to school in the next village. A village school is very different from a school in the town. There are often boys and girls of all ages in the same class. This is not because the older children are stupid but because there are seldom more than two teachers in a village school and big and little children have to be taught together. This is not so difficult as you might think. The older children help the little ones and at the same time they have a chance to hear again things which they may have forgotten.

On the meadow in front of the village a horse dealer is offering to sell his horses to the farmers. One farmer is thinking of buying the white horse. It is brought before him so that he can see whether it is healthy and lively and whether its legs are in good condition.

Most of you know what an English village looks like. The picture shows you a continental village, probably German or Austrian. A farmer lives with his family in the

big white house with the green shutters. The low pink building at the back is the cow-shed. In the steep roof is the hayloft where the winter fodder for the animals is stored. The building on the right is a barn where the corn is kept.

Through the open gate between the cow-shed and the barn you can catch a glimpse of the fields belonging to the farm. There is a large dung heap in front of the cowshed. It has a strong smell but the farmer is pleased because it will help him to keep his land fertile. The two-wheeled machine in the yard is for rooting up potatoes.

The people standing in front are the farmer and his wife, a farmhand and a maid. Country people usually look very healthy because they are all day long in the fresh air.

IN THE COUNTRY

The village you can see in this picture is situated in beautiful scenery close to a large lake, with a view of distant mountains. There is not a single railway or airport or factory to be seen, nothing but trees, meadows and the lake.

People from the town like to come here for their holidays or for the weekend to swim, row or sail or just to go for walks or relax. Some of the villagers take in boarders and a new guest house has recently been built at the water's edge, with a balcony, a terrace and its own bathing beach. Near the guest house is a camping ground for the holiday makers who bring their tents with them.

All through the year the farmers and foresters go about their tasks. The foresters mark the trees which should be cut down, especially those which are getting old or are too near the others for healthy growth to be possible. The woodcutters cut them down with axes or with two-handled saws or power-driven chain saws. Then they trim off the branches.

In the picture, the woodcutters have collected together a number of tall, slender pine trunks and strapped them on a long, flat truck. The tractor driver will take them to the timber-merchant, who will make them into telegraph poles, ships' masts and so on.

You can walk in the woods all day without meeting a single person, even a forester or a woodcutter. If you walk very quietly you may happen upon all kinds of birds and animals, especially towards evening when the deer come out of the forest to feed in the meadows and the hares can be seen jumping about in the fields at the edge of the wood and nibbling the cabbage leaves.

You may, on the other hand, walk for hours without seeing a single creature, though you hardly make as much noise as a mouse. This means that the animals have seen you first and have hidden themselves.

Perhaps you have forgotten what keen eyes wild animals have, and you are wearing rather brightly coloured clothes which can be seen for a long way through the trees. It is for this reason that in countries where there are extensive woods, foresters and sportsmen always dress in green or brown.

In many parts of Europe, especially in Germany, the noble profession of forestry has continued unbroken from ancient times. The forests are as well cared for by the forester as the cornfields and meadows are by the farmer. A good forester will know almost every tree in his preserve. In winter he ensures that, when everything is covered with snow, hay is brought to the feeding places so that the animals of the forest shall not go hungry.

When the forester goes off to work, he takes his axe and saw with him. His wife looks for sticks at the edge of the wood with which to light her fires. As she finds them she piles them in the basket she carries on her back. The gamekeeper takes his gun and dog with him in the hope that he may bring something back for dinner.

A farmhouse near Hamburg

A mountain farm in Switzerland

Cottages in Warwickshire

Farmhouse and olive trees in Spain

THE LANDSCAPE

When a man who has lived all his life in the mountains sees the sea for the first time he gazes in surprise and awe. And anyone who has grown up on the coast is overwhelmed by his first sight of a snow-capped mountain. It is always the scenes which are new and strange that seem the most attractive. But if you travel a great deal, you realise that every variety of landscape has its own charm.

Of all the many types of scenery to be found in the world I have chosen five. Above is a flat coast with a sandy beach. There are sandbanks under the water offshore which are marked by special buoys, in some of which a little hut has been installed as a shelter for the crew of any boat which should get stranded.

The lower picture shows a rocky shore. The tide is just going out. At high tide the sea will come up and cover the entire beach where the man and his little boy are walking.

Of the three kinds of scenery on the page opposite, which would you like to live in if you were allowed to choose?

Flat country

Rolling country

High mountains

THE MAP

The pictures on pages 49 and 50 (the clover crossing and the dam) look very much like maps. For a map is nothing more than a picture of the land seen from the air, rather as a bird sees it or as it appears from an aeroplane. Of course everything is a little simplified on the map, but that is necessary if it is to be clear. Simplification is essential in maps which show vast stretches of country. It would not be possible on such a map to show a town, as it has been drawn here, with all its streets and houses. The town would be marked with a tiny circle or a dot. Details, such as the houses by the sea on this map, would be left out.

It is only necessary to study a map for a short time to understand it. It is particularly easy to follow a coloured map because the colours correspond to those of nature. Rivers, lakes and the sea are coloured blue and where the sea is deepest the blue is darkest. Flat country is shown as green, mountains are coloured brown. Railway lines, roads and motorways can be easily recognised. Buildings are shown in red or black. The black building marked with a cross must be a church and because the open space in front of it is coloured green it must be planted.

Just by the town a river flows into the sea. It is spanned by two bridges, one for road traffic, the other for the railway. The long black building is the railway station. A track runs from the station to the harbour and along the pier. A mole has been built out into the water and there is a lighthouse at the end of it. The brown mountain stretches right to the edge of the sea. At this point the coast is steep and rocky. There are two islands off the shore.

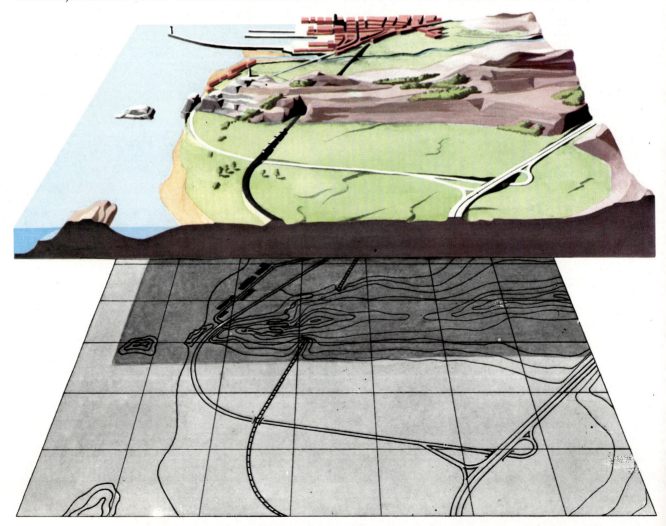

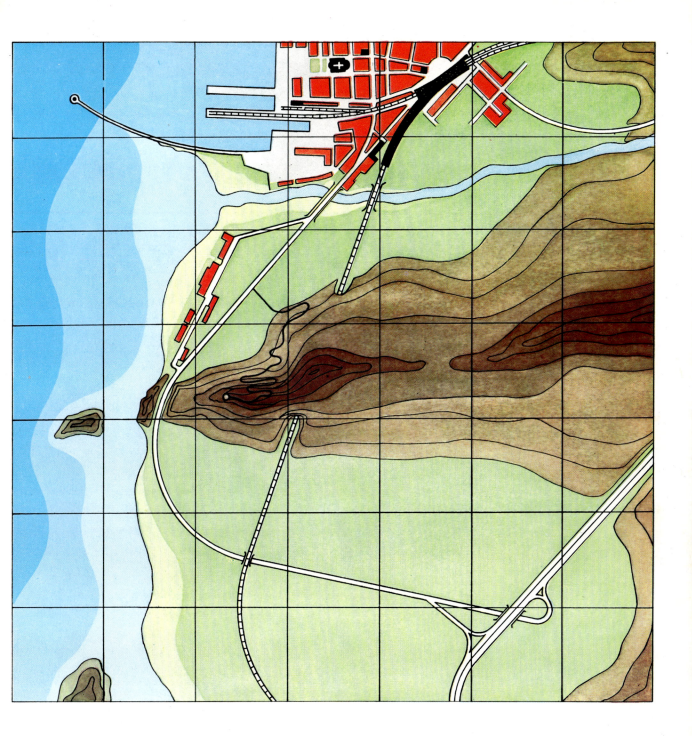

THE COMPASS

If you stand in full sunlight at midday you will cast a shadow. If you turn your back to the sun your shadow will fall directly in front of you towards the north. The south will be directly behind you. To your right lies the east, to your left the west. These are the four points of the compass. Between them lie the north east (NE), the south east (SE), the south west (SW) and the north west (NW).

With a compass it is always possible to find the north even if the sun is not out. The little needle quivering under the glass is made of magnetic iron which has the curious property of always pointing to the north.

65

Reykjavik   ICELAND

FINLAND

NORWAY

Oslo

SWEDEN

Stockholm   Helsinki

NORTH SEA

DENMARK

Copenhagen   BALTIC SEA

EIRE

Dublin   GREAT BRITAIN AND N. IRELAND

POLAND

Warsaw

ATLANTIC OCEAN

London   The Hague   NETHERLANDS   Berlin

BELGIUM   GERMANY

Brussels   Bonn   Prague   CZECHOSLOVAKIA

LUXEMBURG

Luxemburg

Paris

FRANCE   Vienna

Berne   Vaduz   AUSTRIA   HUNGARY   Budapest   ROMANIA

SWITZERLAND   LIECHTENSTEIN

ITALY   Bucharest

Belgrade

YUGOSLAVIA

Monaco   MONACO   San Marino   SAN MARINO

ANDORRA   Sofi

Andorra la Vieja   BULGAR

Lisbon   Madrid   CORSICA   Rome   Tirana   ALBANIA

PORTUGAL   SPAIN   VATICAN CITY   GREECE

SARDINIA

MALLORCA   Athens

SICILY

MEDITERRANEAN SEA

SOVIET UNION

Moscow

This map shows the positions of the various countries, how their frontiers run, the names of the capitals and the national flags. You can see at once how different in size the countries are. If the largest is compared to a giant fruit cake the smallest is no bigger than a raisin

URKEY

CYPRUS

CRETE

EUROPE

Although Europe is small compared with the rest of the world, European ideas have influenced countries as far apart as Africa, Australia and America.

For thousands of years Europe has been able to supply almost all its own needs. It is only fairly recently, with the growth of populations and factories, that we have discovered we cannot produce everything we need and so have to import a great deal of raw material.

The largest country in Europe is the Soviet Union, with its vast production of grain, its advanced technology and scientific achievements. Next comes France, only one-tenth of the size, renowned for fine wines and food as well as for its industries and mines. Spain, nearly as big as France, is another wine-producing country. Then comes Sweden with its great pine forests from which are made matches and paper, and Germany, one of the greatest of the industrialized countries, which also has fairytale castles, good wines and famous musicians.

Italy is another wine-producing country and the north of Italy is the home of car manufacture. Still further north, Finland is a country of lakes and forests and Norway—where the sun shines all day and all night for two months in the summer—has a great fishing industry.

Poland, Romania, Czechoslovakia, Bulgaria and Hungary are all communist countries which work closely with the Soviet Union. They have large agricultural populations, but are building up industries as well.

Great Britain was one of the first great industrial countries, with coal mines, steel works, ports, docks and railways, but a lot of it is still agricultural. The Republic of Eire is also agricultural, becoming more industrialized.

Greece is the country where European civilization and literature really began; Iceland is the home of seafarers and fishermen and Austria has been the birthplace of many wonderful musicians. Denmark is an agricultural country, exporting eggs, bacon and butter to other people; Switzerland, mountainous and beautiful, is the world's banking centre—and makes wonderful chocolate, too! The Dutch are great engineers, who have captured large areas of their land from the sea. Belgium is highly industrialized and there the people speak two languages, French and Flemish. In Luxembourg people speak French and German as well as Luxembourgeios.

Albania, next door to Yugoslavia, is another communist country; little Luxembourg has its own industries as well as producing wine. Lichtenstein, Andorra, Monaco and San Marino are all tiny states and the Vatican City, where the Pope lives, is the smallest of all.

67

ANIMALS

The noblest of all horses are the Arabs and the English racehorses. They are the fastest mounts and are known as thoroughbreds. On no account should they be hitched to a cart or carriage. The best dray horses are the shires but their place has now been almost entirely taken by the lorry and the tractor.

Arab

Racehorse

Shire horse

Carriage horse

Circus pony

Donkey

Cow and bull

Rabbit

Lamb

Sheep

Goat

Pig

St Bernard   Newfoundland

Mastiff

Greyhound

Boxer

Alsatian

Fox Terrier   Scottish Terrier

Dachshund

Poodle

Chow-Chow

Airedale

DOMESTIC ANIMALS

Widely as they differ from each other, all the creatures shown here have one thing in common: they do not have to fend for themselves but are looked after by the people to whom they belong. But they all have to offer something in return. Horses put their strength and their speed at their master's disposal, dogs guard the house or go hunting, cows give milk and sheep wool. Cats catch mice, ducks and hens lay eggs, and geese provide feathers for pillows.

THE DOVECOT

The most beautiful of all the pigeon family is the white fantail dove. She can spread out her tail feathers so that they look like a large white fan. The pouter pigeon puffs up her breast rather as a trumpeter blows out his cheeks.

THE HEN HOUSE

The largest and most beautiful of domestic fowl, the peacock, is sitting on the roof of the henhouse. On his right perches a speckle-breasted guinea hen. Beneath them are two hens and a cock, while three ducks and two geese are waddling up and down in front of the hen house.

Bear, lynx and wolf: in Europe to be found only in the remote forests of Russia and Romania

Badger and raccoon. The badger is really a beast of prey, although when he must he eats roots and leaves. The raccoon eats insects, rodents, frogs, and corn

The opossum has a pouch in which it carries its babies until they are about three months old. Opossums eat mammals and small birds

The marten and the weasel are two small beasts of prey

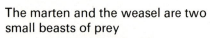

The hare can run as fast as a race-horse. He has long hind legs which enable him to jump over the ground at an amazing rate

The otter lives in a den near rivers and streams and hunts fish. Otters are excellent swimmers. They can also stand up on their hind legs like weasels and stoats. Unlike other beasts of prey, they often kill animals when they are not hungry

WILD ANIMALS

These animals are called wild because they live free and untamed.

Wild animals often suffer great hardship during the winter months and would die of hunger if the foresters did not take fodder to their feeding grounds. Several antlered beasts are to be seen in the picture opposite visiting their feeding ground. On the left is a fallow deer with broad, flattened antlers, while in front of him stands a roebuck with a fawn, a young doe; and on the right you can see a pair of red deer, male and female.

A red squirrel is sitting on the tree. Although he looks rather like a cat he belongs to the same family as do rabbits and rats. He is watching the fox which is sniffing at the track left in the snow by a hare. But by this time the hare must be far away.

There are some animals who spend the winter very comfortably by sleeping right through it. The hamster you can see at the bottom of the picture on the right spends the autumn gathering pounds and pounds of grain which he carries in his pouch-like cheeks to his underground store-chamber. He sits down there the whole winter long, dozing, eating a little now and then and waiting for the spring.

A little higher up there lives a field vole. The gardener hasn't a good word to say for him for he nibbles at the roots of plants. Voles and moles burrow tunnels and chambers under the ground all the year round. The mole (left) has his uses, however, for he eats harmful insects that live in the ground. He is nearly blind but he doesn't mind because he hardly ever comes up to the light of day.

BIRDS

Magpie

If you had eyes as keen as a hawk and you were looking down from a high tower you could read a newspaper spread on the ground. A buzzard circling high above the earth can tell if there is the slightest movement in a molehill down below. He swoops down like a rocket and seizes the poor creature in a flash. All the birds on the left of this page are birds of prey. The great bird at the top is a golden eagle. He looks very noble especially in the air but he is a robber who steals young lambs. He generally builds his nest on a high mountain crag. Just below him a buzzard is sailing through the sky. Near him hovers a kestrel. He hangs twenty or thirty feet above the earth, poised in the air, then slides forward or dives headlong onto his prey. You can recognise him by his long tail. The buzzard and the kestrel can be seen at rest on the old tree stump.

On the lower branch perch three night birds, a short-eared owl, a tawny owl and an eagle owl. All owls spend the day sleeping and dozing. They cannot bear strong light but they can see perfectly in the dark. Their feathers are soft and downy and they fly without making a sound.

The song birds make up a huge family. Many of them, like the swallow, the swift

The cuckoo is named after his call, which you all know. His peculiar habits are described on page 76

The hoopoe looks like a Red Indian. This beautiful bird has disgusting habits. His nest is made of filthy, untidy litter and stinks, and if you annoy him he will spatter you with his droppings

Sparrow
and Starling

and the nightingale, are birds of passage.
When autumn comes they fly in parties
across the Alps to the warmer Mediterranean countries and even as far as Africa.
Some birds of passage however spend the
winter with us and go north in the spring.
Such are the brambling and the yellow-
hammer.

Not all song birds sing well. The best
singers are the nightingale, thrush, blackbird and lark. The wren, the linnet and the
hedge-sparrow can sing sweetly too. But
the house-sparrow can only twitter, while
ravens, rooks and crows do nothing but
croak and cry 'caw, caw' and 'pawk, pawk'.
The starling bubbles, chatters, chuckles and
clicks and can copy the blackbird's song or
the curlew's call.

Wagtail   Plover

On the left of the tree:
Lark
Swallow
Jay
Goldfinch
Bullfinch
Robin
Nuthatch
Spotted woodpecker

On the right of the tree:
Thrush
Blackbird
Chaffinch
Nightingale
Blue tit
Long-tailed tit
Kingfisher

Wren    Crow

Reed warbler, heron and, flying overhead, a peewit or lapwing

Two grey geese, teal, mallard and, flying overhead, two storks

CUCKOO'S EGGS

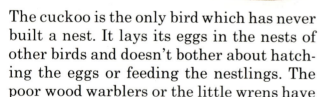

The cuckoo is the only bird which has never built a nest. It lays its eggs in the nests of other birds and doesn't bother about hatching the eggs or feeding the nestlings. The poor wood warblers or the little wrens have to look after them though they have more than enough to do with their own brood. When the young cuckoo is hatched he grows very fast and is soon bigger than his foster parents. He is often so greedy that he pushes the other young ones out of the nest. And in spite of that his foster parents go on patiently feeding him until he is big enough to fly away.

A wood warbler feeding a young cuckoo

Song bird nestling

Peewit chick

Coot chick

An eider duck in flight and a crested grebe with chicks

Coots, a mute swan and overhead a curlew

NESTLINGS AND CHICKS

When a young song bird hatches out of the egg he is very small and has no feathers. The biggest thing about him is his beak and his feet are far too big for his body. He can't see and he can't walk, he can't do anything but eat and eat, and if he falls out of the nest he will certainly die. He just has to stay in the nest and eat the food his mother brings him and wait until his feathers grow. The chicks of game birds and many water fowl can run as soon as they are hatched and are covered with soft down, though of course they cannot fly until they have grown wings.

Not all water birds can swim. The long-legged stork and heron wade near the bank and look for food on the bottom of the stream.

Male and female grouse

Pheasant

When they are swimming upstream, trout and salmon will jump over weirs and rapids. There are three kinds of trout shown here of which the bottom one is the rainbow trout. The large fish to the right is a salmon. When the young salmon hatch out in fresh water, they swim down to the sea and only return to the river to spawn

The pike perch and the common perch (top) are only found in the larger rivers. At the bottom is a huge catfish 6 to 9 feet in length. In the foreground is an eel and down in the corner are two freshwater mussels

POND AND RIVER LIFE

Fish, shrimps, tadpoles, shellfish and snails are but some of the many kinds of creature which live in fresh water. Some prefer still water, some a strong current. Trout are fond of fast-flowing streams. Catfish are found in rivers while the carp lives in a lake or a pond.

Fish deposit their eggs, or spawn, in clutches on the bottom of streams or ponds.

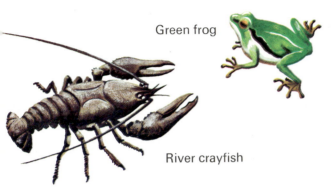

Green frog

River crayfish

The pike is a great hunter and feeds on fish, frogs, toads, newts, water voles, rats and even young water fowl. The crayfish is a river scavenger for he eats everything, even dead animals. But many fish, the carp among them, live only on plants and small water insects.

The eel and the salmon are both great travellers. The salmon leaves the sea to spawn in the river while the eel journeys from fresh water to the sea, and then sometimes more than a thousand miles to lay her eggs and die. The young eels swim back to the river after living for about three years in the sea.

The little stickleback, unlike other fish, builds a domed nest out of the roots and stems of waterplants and defends its young.

On the top is a carp, below it a pike and at the bottom, a water snail and a stickleback

79

SEA CREATURES

Sea Horse

Starfish

Tellen

Whelk

At the top a jellyfish or medusa, below, a cuttlefish and bottom, a crab and a hercules crab

Nineteen different creatures are shown on these two pages but they represent only a minute proportion of all the thousands of fascinating inhabitants of the great oceans. Naturalists probably still do not know all the varieties of sea life, for in some places the water is as deep as the mountains are high. It was not until a few years ago that it became possible to explore the deepest waters by means of the bathyscaphe. Creatures were then discovered which never come anywhere near the surface.

Many sea creatures look so strange to us at first sight that it is difficult to believe they are animals. Sea anemones, starfish, polyps and squids look more like flowers than creatures. The cuttlefish has a number of arms or tentacles which look as though they were growing out of the top of its head and it can squirt out an inky liquid in order to darken the water around it and so baffle its enemies. Its eggs are sometimes found lying on the seashore looking just like bunches of purple grapes.

The largest of all sea creatures is the whale, It is not a fish and it does not lay eggs; its young are born alive. This sea monster is 45 to 60 feet long and weighs as much as 200 large bulls. At the top of the page opposite you can see what a whaler looks like and how the whale is harpooned. Fat and oil are extracted from the dead beast once it is on board the whaler. Now so many whales have been killed that most nations agree that they should not be hunted so much.

In the days when there were no steam or motor-driven boats whales were hunted from rowing boats. The harpoons, which are now fired from a whaling gun, were then thrown by hand, a most dangerous practice. The boat had to approach the whale very closely and if the harpoon was not very skilfully aimed the whole crew might lose their lives. A whale that was not killed might smash the boat to atoms with a single blow of his mighty tail.

Fleet of
whalers

Sperm
Whale
(65 ft)

Blue Whale
(95 ft)

Blue Shark
(25 ft)

Spotted
Dogfish
(15ft)

Sword Fish
(10 ft)

Thornback
Ray (15 ft)

Tunny Fish
(5 ft)

Sturgeon
(6 ft)

Gurnard
($1\frac{1}{2}$ ft)

Plaice
($2\frac{1}{2}$ ft)

Herring

REPTILES

Lizards, snakes and tortoises belong to this group. They all, especially the first two, love the heat of the sun and spend hours basking on warm rocks. But at the slightest sound they become alert, the tortoise retires into his shell and the snake and lizard dart away at lightning speed. At the top right of the picture opposite is a tortoise from Greece and below it a viper with a poisonous bite. On the left is a grass snake. In the middle is a common lizard, below it a green lizard and at the bottom a blindworm. A toad, an amphibian like the frog, sits in the shade of a rock.

AMPHIBIANS

These creatures are born and pass the early part of their lives in the water, when they breathe through gills. Then they take to the land, and breathe with lungs. But they always have to stay close to a pond or stream and must return there to lay their eggs. Below, for instance, is shown a tree frog. Its large cluster of eggs, all laid at the same time, cling together in a frothy mass called frog spawn. The little black dot in the centre of each globe of jelly grows bigger and bigger until, after three or four weeks, a small black wriggling tadpole comes out. Just behind its round head short feathery gills begin to sprout. Then after a time a small swelling appears on each side of the tail and these develop into a pair of hind legs. Nine or ten weeks after being hatched the tadpole sheds its gills and grows two forelegs. It still has a tail but this gets shorter and shorter until it disappears. The tadpole has become a frog.

The chameleon, a tree lizard, is an astonishing creature that lives (for example) in southern Spain. He is very good at catching flies and gnats. His actual colour is green but he can change it in the twinkling of an eye. When he is close to rocks he will become grey, red or striped. He also changes colour if he is hungry or thirsty or excited. He lies for the most part absolutely motionless on a branch. Only his protruding eyes are alive and look around for insects. Then suddenly there is a flicker of his long, sticky tongue and his prey is caught.

The salamander has a tail like a newt. In contrast to the agile frog he moves quite slowly. He has no need to hurry for if another animal tries to seize him, the glands in his skin give off a bitter tasting fluid which is so poisonous that it can kill small animals.

INSECTS

Insects have bodies which are clearly divided into three: head, middle, called the thorax, and a larger hind part called the abdomen. The legs are attached to the thorax and are never more than six in number. Above the eyes are two long feelers looking like two pieces of thread. By the delicate sense of touch which these feelers possess the insect can tell what is good to eat. Insects pass through strange changes in their lives. The history of the common cabbage white is typical. It lays its eggs on a cabbage leaf. In a few days a tiny caterpillar will hatch from each egg. This little grub feeds on the cabbage, grows bigger and bigger and after a few weeks crawls to a crack in a wall where it attaches itself by means of a pad of silk at the tail and a loop of silk across its middle—the silk being made by glands in the mouth. The skin of its back then bursts to show the horny body of a chrysalis. It remains fixed until the butterfly emerges and unfolds its wings.

Purple Emperor

Swallowtail

Apollo

Peacock

Red Admiral

White Nun

Monarch

Cabbage white with caterpillar and chrysalis

Magpie Moth

Tiger Moth

BEETLES

The smallest beetles are so tiny that several can stand together on a pin's head. Yet they have everything that a beetle should have: six legs, a pair of hard, horny wings (which serve as cases for the transparent hind wings folded beneath them), strong biting jaws and a pair of long feelers made up of several joints. Nearly all beetles have the whole body covered by a thick, tough coat which forms a hard protective armour.

The largest of all European insects is the stag beetle. Only in Brazil are some insects larger still. It lives in woods and should not be taken by collectors as it has become rare, so much so that it is in danger of dying out. The larva lives in burrows in oak and ash trees, feeding on the wood. It takes a long time to grow and is easily disturbed. If this happens it becomes a pupa too soon and the beetle which eventually emerges is often too weak to lay eggs. The huge jaws of the male stag beetle are used as weapons for fighting.

Except for the death's head moth insects have no voices. But crickets produce a chirping sound by rubbing one horny wing-case against the other, and the grasshopper emits a shrill note by rubbing its jumping legs against the inner sides of its wing-case.

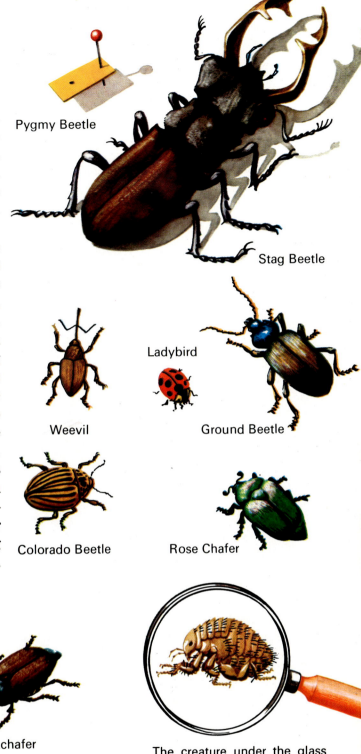

Pygmy Beetle

Stag Beetle

Weevil

Ladybird

Ground Beetle

Colorado Beetle

Rose Chafer

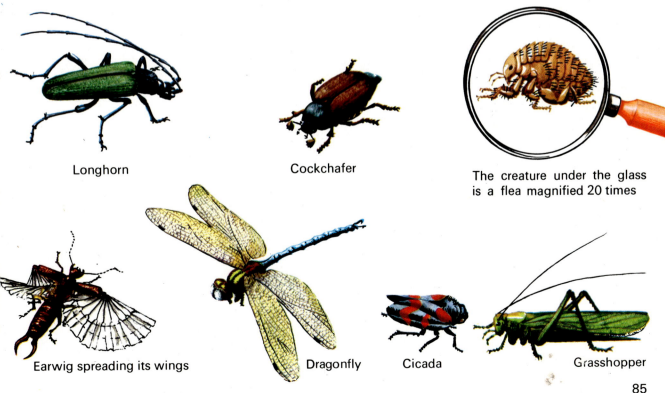

Longhorn

Cockchafer

The creature under the glass is a flea magnified 20 times

Earwig spreading its wings

Dragonfly

Cicada

Grasshopper

85

feed the larvae and collect food, while the queen gives all her attention to laying eggs. Honey bees, which lay up stores for the winter, can survive from year to year, but, except for the young queens which have been reared in the nest, and which sleep in sheltered holes through the cold months, all the inmates of a bumble bee colony die after the first sharp frost of autumn.

On the left you will see a honeycomb in a beehive. The dark cells are empty, others, in which eggs are hatching, are sealed with wax. Some of the cells are full of golden yellow honey. The large cell at the bottom is the nursery of a queen bee. She is just crawling out and this is a signal for the old queen to found a new colony somewhere else. The swarms of bees which are sometimes seen in summer consist of a queen who has left her home accompanied by a host of drones and workers. As soon as she settles, her followers cluster closely about her in a solid mass and the whole swarm may then be collected and introduced into a new hive.

Soon afterwards the queen chooses a drone to be her partner in the marriage flight. For the whole of the rest of the summer she lays eggs at the rate of one a minute. She is the only bee that is able to lay eggs. Most of the drones are either bitten or stung to death after the nuptial flight for they are of no further use to the colony as they do not work.

BEES

The beehive hums with the sound of three kinds of bees: the queen, an immense number of workers and a few hundred drones, which are all male. Honey bees provide us with honey which they manufacture from the nectar of flowers, and also with wax from their glands. The bees use the wax to make six-sided cells joined together to form a honey-comb. The queen bee lays her eggs in these cells, or they are used to store honey for the winter. During the cold season, bee-keepers give their bees sugar, which they like just as much as honey. Bees live not only on nectar but also on pollen. And as they go from flower to flower they perform a most useful service by carrying the pollen from one to the other—pollen which the new seeds must have before they can grow.

Bees lead a very orderly life, governed by definite laws. The worker bees build cells,

WASPS

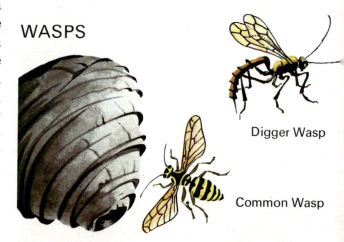

Digger Wasp

Common Wasp

Many wasps live in colonies, making their nests of particles of wood mixed with saliva, but the digger wasp lives all alone.

ANTS

Ants belong to the same group of insects as do bees and wasps. There are many different kinds of ants living in woods, in hill-sides, under paving stones and even in our houses. The red ants that live in woods bite fiercely if you disturb their nests, but they are very useful creatures, the enemies of many harmful caterpillars which would eat up whole forests if the ants were not there to check them. Thousands of ants including as many as a hundred large females live in one nest. The nest consists of a number of separate chambers and halls connected by a wonderful system of galleries with passages and streets leading to the outside world. When the females first develop they have wings. There are also a number of large males which are winged. Mating takes place in the air between these winged males and females. On coming to rest the females bite off their wings, for they will never need them again, and they at once begin to lay eggs. They go on laying eggs for the rest of their lives, some 15 or 20 years. The small wingless workers, such as you see running busily over paths, do all the work of building, storing, cleaning the nest and tending the larvae.

On the right you see the inside of an ants' nest such as is usually found in a heap of soil or underground. At the very bottom a female is laying eggs. A little higher up you will notice some larvae and higher still some cocoons, the so-called ants' eggs which are sold as food for gold-fish. The creature with which the two ants on the right are busy is a plant louse. These insects are captured by the ants and kept for the sake of sweet syrup called honey dew which comes from glands in their hind-quarters, The ants take great care of their charges, tending them as a farmer does his cows.

In fact "ant-cows" is another name for the plant-lice, because of the way the ants look after them and "milk" them.

The hind part of the ant makes a pouch for food storage. When the ant returns to the nest the food it has gathered is used to nourish the larvae and the females.

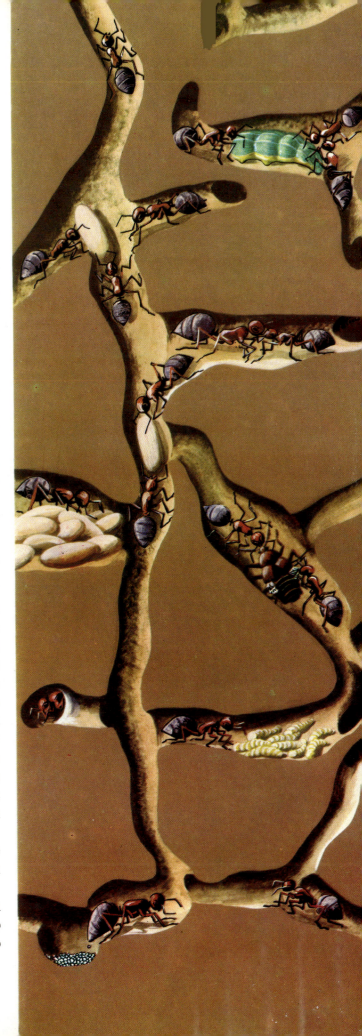

PLANTS

VEGETABLES

Generally speaking, animals are divided into two kinds—the ones who eat vegetables and fruits and the ones who eat meat. Occasionally a meat-eating animal will eat green stuff, but vegetarian animals don't touch meat. Man is the only animal who seems happy with either. Eskimos, for instance, remain perfectly healthy on a diet of nothing but meat, fish and fat; but

there are lots of people everywhere who think it is wrong to kill animals for food and who eat only vegetables and fruit.

If he wants to keep healthy, a man's food must include various different substances and some of the most important ones are called vitamins and are found a lot in fruit and vegetables. They are tiny, tasteless particles named after the letters of the alphabet and each one has a different job to do. So although you could live on meat only and get the necessary vitamins, it might be

Pumpkin

Cucumber   Chicory   White Radish   Leek   Celeriac   Cauliflower   Spinach

Radish   Peas   Broad Beans   Aubergine   Artichoke   Red Pepper

BERRIES AND GRAPES

Left, garden strawberries; below, currants, which can also be black or white. Centre, gooseberries. On the right is a cluster of grapes. A lot of people like the wine made from grape juice very much and many countries have vineyards where grapes are grown to make wine.

rather dull; it is more interesting to eat fruit and vegetables as well. It is fortunate that there are so many kinds of vegetable and that some of them can be stored for the winter. It is always better to eat fresh vegetables because they contain the most vitamins. And with the help of greenhouses gardeners are able to grow fresh vegetables in very early spring and late autumn. Some greenhouses, like the large one shown in the picture opposite, can be heated, but this is only necessary in winter. In spring and autumn the glass roof provides sufficient protection against the cold night air. Less delicate plants can be reared in frames like the ones you can see in front of the greenhouse, with glass that can be lifted off.

Vegetable gardens must be well watered and sometimes have a wind-driven pump.

More than two dozen varieties of vegetables are shown here and these are only a few of those that exist. Some, such as cabbages and potatoes, do not have to be grown either in greenhouse or in a frame.

Asparagus   Fennel   Tomato   Lettuce   Carrot   Kohlrabi

Cabbage   Onion   Brussels sprouts   Horseradish   Potato

Red Clover

Trefoil

Beetroot

Sugar Beet

FIELD CROPS

The gardener concerns himself with fruit and vegetables but everything grown in the open fields is looked after by the farmer. The farmer's work is neither easier nor harder than that of the gardener: it is different. The gardener has more trouble in rearing his plants while the farmer is busier at seed time and harvest. He also has to look after his cattle as well as his crops. So he grows not only what is good for man but also food for his animals, crops such as clover, for instance, which is important for cattle. There are more kinds of clover than those shown here, and there are other crops which make excellent fodder: vetch, lucerne and all the varieties of grass. Of the root crops, the turnip is used as fodder and the sugar beet yields sugar when it is treated in factories.

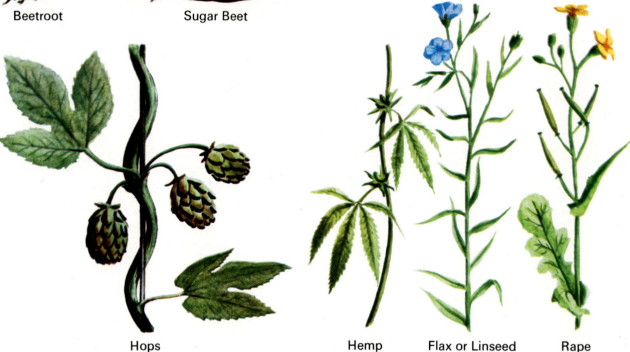

Hops

Hemp   Flax or Linseed   Rape

Hop growers have to erect long poles and wires in their fields so that the hops, which are climbing plants, can grow really high—so high that the men who tend them have to walk on stilts. The fruit, with the addition of yeast and barley, is used for brewing beer.

In addition to the hop, hemp, flax and rape are shown here. Every kind of rope from

string to thick cord is made from hemp fibres. Hemp seeds produce oil which is used in making soap, and they also make excellent bird food. The flax too is a hairy plant, but the hairs are much finer. They are used to make linen, while the seeds supply the painter's linseed oil. The rape stem is not hairy but the seeds are rich in oil.

CEREALS

This page shows some of the most important kinds of corn which can be cultivated in open fields, best of all in fields which are flat, for there the work of scattering the seed and gathering in the harvest is easiest. Apart from good soil, corn needs nothing in order to grow but favourable weather, sun and rain in early summer, sun at the height of the season and no rain just before the harvest, which should be dry when it is gathered. Behind the ears of corn you can see a large threshing-machine which beats the grains from the ears and tips them into sacks. The empty ears and the stalks are chopped up to make cheap although not very nourishing fodder for sheep and cattle.

Rye   Wheat   Barley   Oats   Millet

GARDEN FLOWERS

In fine summer weather the garden is like an extra part of the house—a new room which makes a great deal of work. But it is very healthy work, particularly for town dwellers whose usual work is so different, and it is the kind of work people enjoy doing.

Most of the plants in town gardens are fine ornamental flowers of which new varieties are continually being produced. Especially in Holland there are nurseries which are famous for the cultivation of roses, tulips, lilies and all bulb plants and from which seeds and bulbs are sent to garden lovers all over the world.

Many people grow their own lettuces. They also grow fruit trees and fruit bushes and keep a herb garden. Their garden is almost like a miniature farm, cultivated for the needs of themselves and their friends.

Hyacinth   Daffodil   Tulip

Iris   Gladiolus   Lily

WILD FLOWERS

Violet

Kingcup

Snowdrop

Anemone

Daisy

Windflower

Cowslip

Wild Thyme

Lily of the Valley

Campanula

Maiden Pink

Larkspur

Cornflower

Poppy

Meadow Saffron

96

Dandelion   Purple Orchis   Columbine   Oxeye Daisy   Vetch   Turk's Cap Lily

ALPINE FLOWERS

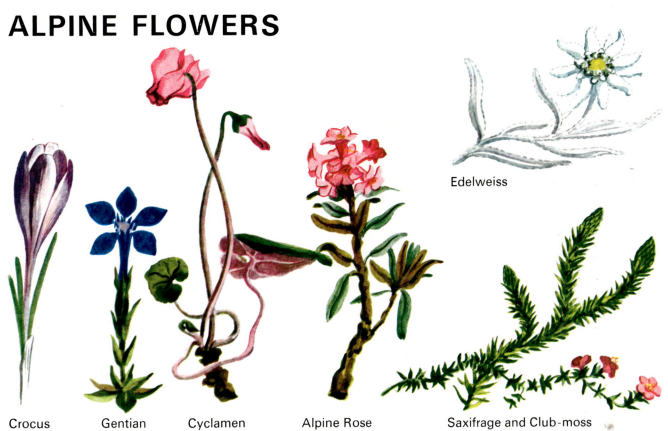

Edelweiss

Crocus   Gentian   Cyclamen   Alpine Rose   Saxifrage and Club-moss

97

Wild Strawberry   Bilberry   Cranberry

Raspberry   Blackberry   Red Whortleberry

BERRIES AND HERBS

Many hermits, according to legend, are supposed to have lived on nothing but wild berries and nuts. They must always have felt rather hungry and unsatisfied!

There are all kinds of other plants growing in the woods and on the heath which are no more satisfying than berries if you are hungry but which are nevertheless important for their healing properties. A concoction of coltsfoot leaves is good for a cough and watercress is good for kidney trouble. The juice of nettles helps chilblains. Valerian is said to cure cramp and palpitations. Camomile relieves sore gums and a bad cold. Arnica helps sprains and bruises; woodruff, they say, improves the temper!

Coltsfoot   Platain   Woodruff   Valerian   Centaury   Camomile   Arnica

FUNGI

Fungi, or mushrooms and toadstools, have neither flowers nor leaves like other plants and new ones grow from spores instead of seeds. The spore starts growing in the ground and puts out a delicate filament as fine as a cobweb which gradually becomes a mesh of gossamer-like threads. These threads are almost invisible in the earth but they can sometimes be seen in the fluffy mould on bread or jam. From them grow two sorts of fungi, some of which have an appetizing smell and are good to eat and others which are evil smelling and poisonous. The fungi which you can eat are much enjoyed as vegetables and for making soup. Some people find it more exciting to look for mushrooms than to eat them and they are ready to get up at dawn to be the first in the fields or woods, for mushrooms are supposed to come up suddenly in the night. They do indeed grow very quickly especially after rain. Many people believe that only mushrooms are edible but a number of fungi of the toadstool kind are nonpoisonous and have been eaten for more than 3000 years. But, only pick those you *know* to be good.

Field Mushroom   Truffle   Cep

Parasol Mushroom   Chanterelle   Saffron Milk Cap

Brown Toad   Button Mushroom

Wood Mushroom   Fairy Ring Champignon   Orange Cap Boletus   Lurid Boletus   Wooly Milk Cap   Dotted Stem Boletus

BEWARE!

The fungi on the right are all poisonous. First is the Death Cup, the most dangerous of all. It has no smell. Next are the Gyromitra and the Devil's Boletus. Last come two Agarics, old and young. Beware of other poisonous fungi!

Lime · Oak · Beech · Elm

TREES

Furniture, floors, rafters, window frames and doors, step ladders, carts, bridges, fences, tools and goods of all kinds are made of wood from trees. And in addition to these, many other tings are made—paper and certain dress fabric for instance—which you would never guess came from wood.

Wood was formerly used even more widely than it is today. For a long time it supplied most of the fuel for cooking and heating and for these purposes far more wood was needed than was provided by fallen trees. More wood was also used for building houses as well as ships. So it came about that in nearly every country the forests became smaller and smaller. Trees grow to a great height but it takes a long time and very often the people who cut the trees down never thought of planting new ones. At first they did not notice what was happening to the ground where the trees had stood and when they did it was almost too late. The soil had become dry and cracked, the rocks had been laid bare by rain and melting snow, and there was nothing to break the force of the wind as it swept across the land. Gradually the soft rich loam where the forest had once stood was changed into an exposed stony tract where nothing could take root, because all the soil had been blown or swept away and the rainwater drained away too quickly. The few saplings which sprang up here and there were bent and beaten by the wind and soon withered, for they were no longer protected by older trees. This could have been avoided if a new tree had been planted for every one felled.

Trees are of two kinds: deciduous and evergreen. The leaves of deciduous trees turn yellow and red in the autumn and fall off, leaving the tree bare until the following spring. Evergreens include conifers like the fir, the pine and the yew, which have dark green needles instead of leaves. These are continuously renewed as they fall off, so that the trees are never bare but remain green all through the winter, which is probably why the fir has been chosen as the tree for Christmas. The larch is peculiar in that it is a conifer but not an evergreen. Its needles turn brown in the autumn and drop off. The ilex, too, is unusual—it is an evergreen but not a conifer, and has thick shiny leaves rather like the holly.

Birch

Maple

Ash

Alder

Willow

Pine

Fir

Scots Pine

Larch

Yew

Cypress

Juniper

101

Apple

Pear

TREE FRUITS

Fruit is the easiest of all things to eat. You can pick it ripe from the tree and it is ready at once. That is what makes it so tempting to trespass in someone else's garden and climb a tree. But is it really worth all the trouble? You usually tear your clothes and have to run for it and you nearly always have to throw away the apple before you have had more than one or two bites!

Fruit is as important as vegetables for food because it is full of the vitamins mentioned a page or two back. The riper and fresher the fruit the better it is. Some kinds of fruit, such as apples and the harder varieties of pear, will keep fresh for a long time.

Some years are good for fruit, others are bad. If there is frost at night after the tree has blossomed the tender flowers will be

Cherries

Plums

Peach

Apricot

Orange

Lemon

Fig

Olives

killed off and not even the warmest, longest summer can save the fruit. Or if the weather gets cold too early in the autumn the fruit will not ripen. Fruit trees require calm showery weather in spring, a sunny summer and a warm autumn, particularly in northern Europe. In the south, in the Mediterranean countries, where oranges, lemons, figs, olives and almonds grow, it is different. The summer there is much longer.

Sweet Chestnut

Walnut

Hazelnut

Almond

THROUGH THE AGES

UP TO 10,000 YEARS AGO

Some ten thousand years ago two children, wandering by chance into an old deserted cave, saw the walls were covered with painted pictures. "I wonder who did that? Perhaps it was uncle or one of our great-uncles." They couldn't imagine a longer time than that. Nobody thought of the past or the future then, and every day was spent searching for food and for shelter from the wind, rain and snow. People realised that a man could not deal with the dangers of life alone, so they lived in family groups and tribes, just like the animals around them in flocks and herds. They also copied the animals by finding caves and sleeping on beds of leaves and dry grass instead of on the hard ground.

But men already lived better than animals. They could make tools out of stone, wood and bones and they had discovered how to make fire by striking flints together. They could also make clay pots. They could not write but they did draw and paint. The earliest cave pictures were probably done much longer ago than 10,000 years. The colours were made from earth and plant juices.

These cave paintings were rediscovered in 1879. A Spaniard from a place called Altamira saw an exhibition of prehistoric tools and weapons in Paris. He knew of some caves near his estate in Spain, so he explored them for more of these old tools. He took his little daughter aged five with him and she was the first person to see the red and black pictures on the walls, as she wandered around, carrying the lantern.

Stone hammer and flint knife

Clay pots and a bone comb

Spear with bone point

Fish trap made of plaited willow

Huts built on the edge of a lake. In the foreground a thatched stone hut

Soon afterwards, many more cave paintings were found in Spain, France and Italy. Most of them show hunting or fishing scenes, and there is a drawing of two men smoking out a bees' nest. In some of the pictures even houses can be seen and in one of them there is a plough and a cart drawn by oxen. The strange signs and symbols often cut in the rock were perhaps believed to ward off evil spirits.

Without realising it the ancient cave painters were recording the story of their lives for the future. Their pots, tools and weapons found lying in the ground and the objects they put in their graves, tell us still more about them, their customs and their skill as craftsmen.

Clay box shaped like a house for keeping the ashes of the dead

4,500 years old
Egyptian pyramid, temple and obelisk

3,300 years old
Grave mound of an ancient Greek king

UP TO 2,000 YEARS AGO

The things you see on these pages happened during the eight thousand years after the things on the page you have just turned over. In some parts of the world people went on living in exactly the same way as the cave painters. But in the Mediterranean and Near Eastern countries a great change came about. Men had discovered the uses of metal and were turning it into weapons, pots and ornaments. Copper and tin, when melted together, were found to make a new metal, bronze, which could be shaped into knives, saws, nails and clasps. The discovery of iron was even more important and iron became even more precious than gold. Gold was beautiful, but iron was hard and from it men learned how to forge steel.

The men of 2,000 years ago had long been traders. They bartered and bought metalwork, pottery and glass and woven woollen cloth which was finer than their coarse linen. The Sumerians, people from lower Mesopotamia, and the Egyptians had both invented ways of writing and had begun to record their histories. Great cities grew up, where there were temples, harbours, running water and drains, schools, libraries and public baths. There were religious festivals and public shows and people kept slaves to look after them and to work for them. The ruins of ancient buildings in Egypt, Greece and Italy help to give us an idea of how people once lived, worked and worshipped in those places.

Egyptian sculptor carving an inscription

Greek lady at a loom

2,500 years old
Greek temple

1,900 years old
Roman Triumphal Arch: Roman Aqueduct

Up till this time most of the progress made by the human race had been through the cleverness and enterprise of the Near Eastern peoples, like the Hittites, Sumerians, Phoenicians and Egyptians. But 2,000 years ago, a little time before the birth of Christ, the empires which these peoples had ruled had faded away. The Near East and the whole of Europe westwards as far as Spain and northwards as far as the British Isles, was under the rule of the Romans. The Romans built roads which are still used today and they established their own law and order in every country they went to, including distant lands like Britain, where people still lived in tribes.

Modern civilization started with these

Greek Chariot

ancient peoples. From them we inherited a knowledge of how to manufacture steel and glass, of the wheel and the plough, of spinning, weaving, mathematics and astronomy. Science and philosophy began with them.

Greek Minstrel

Roman lady and gentleman

Celtic peasants from Gaul (France)

UP TO 1,000 YEARS AGO

Many cities all over the civilized world were burned down by wild tribes like the Goths and Vandals from central and eastern Europe and the Huns, from Asia, great horsemen who swept in under their chief Attila. By the end of the fifth century local kings, often not much different from brigand chieftains, were reigning in most of western and central Europe. In the south the Arabs spread their rule, religion and language from North Africa across the sea as far as Spain. Later on pirates from the far north, the Norsemen raided all the coasts of Europe down to Spain and eventually made a home in the north of France, which therefore got the name of Normandy.

Now and again during these dangerous centuries there arose rulers with the courage and determination to make some sort of order around them. One of these was the Emperor Charlemagne and another was Alfred the Great. Christianity was the religion of half Europe; monasteries had been founded everywhere and kept art and knowledge alive in the midst of the fighting and lawlessness all around. Without the history books which the monks kept up to date and the old manuscripts which they carefully copied we should know less than we do about the world of the Greeks and Romans, and the times that followed.

Historians have given this period the name the Dark Ages, and call the style of the buildings Romanesque because of the rounded doors, windows and arches, copied from the round arches of the ancient Romans.

The picture shows a settlement close to a monastery such as could be found 1,000 years ago in all Christian lands. Many of these settlements developed later into important towns

A room in the Romanesque style in a bishop's palace

UP TO 500 YEARS AGO

Gradually life became safer and more settled but times were not peaceful. The power of the church had steadily increased with the spread of Christianity and so the Pope and bishops came into conflict with the emperors, kings and princes. However, about 800 years ago when the crusaders were setting out from France, England and Germany to free the holy city of Jerusalem from the Muslim Arabs and Turks, Christendom came near to being united for a while at the call of the Pope. But on the whole the crusades were not very successful and eventually Jerusalem fell once more into the hands of the Muslims.

It was a hard life for the knights on crusades. They did indeed travel far and they saw the wonders of foreign lands but in comparison with the rich and civilized princes of the East they seemed to be no better than rough countrymen gone soldiering. They brought home many rare and costly things from the east, fine silks, perfumes and beautiful jewellery. They planted peach trees from Persia in their gardens and they grew strange new vegetables such as spinach. But finding the money to go out on these many expeditions with arms, horses and soldiers led to heavy debts for the knights. So they offered their services to the rich princes who could pay them well and they rented their land to the peasants, demanding complete control over their tenants' lives.

The churches and great houses began to be built in a new, fashionable style called Gothic. Windows, doors and arches were all pointed, tall pillars soared up to the roofs and there were slender turrets and lofty pointed steeples. Beautiful windows, made of stone tracery almost as fine as lace, were filled with glowing glass pictures in all colours. Everything was pointed, even gentlemen's shoes and ladies' headdresses.

All the time the world was changing. Already many people could read and write. There were scholars and great libraries apart from those in the monasteries. These

times were called the Middle Ages and lasted until about 500 years ago.

A man in Germany, called Johannes Gutenberg, had invented printing with moveable metal letters. Books and reading encouraged knowledge and aroused curiosity about the world beyond Europe. Men began to write books to be read by quite ordinary people. And they wrote in the languages that people spoke as well as in Latin. The kind of life we lead now began to take shape during the Middle Ages.

UP TO 400 YEARS AGO

Wars and disturbances continued to trouble the people of Europe, and with the invention of gunpowder war seemed to have become even more terrible. In earlier days men fought to take land and power from their neighbours, now they also fought to make them accept different opinions. It was the time of the Reformation. Many Bibles had been printed and for the first time people could read the scriptures for themselves. Many of the inhabitants of northern Europe broke away from the Roman Catholic Church and the quarrel soon took the form of war between the rulers. Of course some rulers cared very little for religious freedom and only fought because they thought they might gain some personal advantage by it. They hired bands of soldiers called mercenaries (from a Latin word, *mercenarius*, meaning reward) who were willing to fight for anyone who paid them well.

This was also an age of exploration for riches as well as of wars for opinions. Christopher Columbus crossed the Atlantic in 1492; Sir Francis Drake sailed round the world in 1580 and a Portuguese, Magellan had led the way about 60 years earlier.

People became aware of strange lands, animals and plants, manners and customs.

A mercenary from
Switzerland or Germany

Delicacies and materials were brought to Europe: silk and tea from China, coffee, cane sugar, rice and rare spices from Asia, tobacco and cotton from North America and a root from South America—the potato.

The first discoverers and conquerors came from Spain, Portugal and Italy, and they were followed by the English, the Dutch and the French, who explored, traded and colonized all over the world. New riches flowed into Europe from overseas, while in Italy a new kind of thought, which we call the Renaissance ('new birth') was beginning.

The English
fashion

The Spanish
fashion

Courtyard of a French château

UP TO 300 YEARS AGO

With the period called the Renaissance came a new knowledge and appreciation of the achievements of the ancient Greeks and Romans, which had been forgotten for so long. New buildings were designed to look like Greek or Roman temples and palaces. The soaring, pointed arches and spires of the Gothic style went right out of fashion and with the new style of building came new ideas on every conceivable subject.

From Italy, the home of the Renaissance, the movement spread over the whole of Europe. It took a long time to get to the British Isles and had scarcely arrived before it was followed by another new style—also from Italy—which was called Baroque. It was named after a Spanish word meaning an irregularly-shaped pearl, and was both luxurious and elaborate.

Towns, palaces and country houses became more and more splendid, but the times were just as disturbed as ever. Wars for conquest or for religion still went on, but there were wars about power in individual countries. After periods of destruction, peace would return, under a new ruler.

The Thirty Years War, the worst war in Europe until modern times, started in Prague, because the Catholic emperor in Vienna did not want a Protestant king in Bohemia. Soon the struggle involved many kingdoms, even Sweden, and became less about religion and more about power. It spread over Germany, France, Holland and Belgium, and even to Italy and Spain. Meanwhile, in the British Isles, the civil war between the king and Parliament was turning the country upside down. The French were also at war during this period, and in addition, the Turks, who had captured the Balkans, attacked Vienna.

But once all the fighting was over, people quickly went back to normal. They rebuilt their homes, better than before. Their new bridges were stronger, their roads firmer, their churches more sumptuous. Reasonable people somehow managed to come into their own after all the cruelty and folly. It is a hopeful sign when one sees that in difficult times like those, clever men not only became gunsmiths and armourers, but also turned to making pocket watches, to writing and printing books, to grinding lenses for spectacles and telescope lenses.

A mercenary soldier, a Dutchman and his wife standing in front of a castle

The thrifty French finance minister, Etienne de Silhouette, gave his name to silhouettes. He himself cut them out as a hobby. It was a way of making portraits without paying an expensive artist and it became the fashion to have these shadow-outlines of one's family and friends

UP TO 200 YEARS AGO

So nations grew; sometimes they grew by chance, sometimes thanks to a great ruler's good sense. Their own riches were often increased by possessions over the seas. The longer there was peace, the more prosperous a country's citizens became, as trade could then prosper all the time. Towns became grander, houses became more comfortable. Streets were being paved, and in some very rich quarters, they were even lit up at night. Now it was the turn of the gorgeous Baroque style to be replaced by a more lighthearted and delicate style, called Rococo, perhaps from a French name for a collection of pebbles and shells. Buildings and rooms and furniture were elegantly decorated with shapes like those, and so got the name.

Life in general was being made nicer. There was more comfort, and a little more cleanliness. Clothes were made of softer stuffs. Porcelain was in use, and people ate with knives and forks, instead of with their fingers. The rich people took to wearing wigs.

To have more than enough of everything can lead to boredom, and the idle and wealthy began to take up all sorts of odd ideas. They took an interest in the countryside and the beauties of nature, but they only looked at the pretty side and ignored the poverty and unhappiness. Fine ladies and gentlemen from the French Court dressed up as countryfolk and played at being milkmaids and shepherd boys. The birds, brooks and flowers gave them a lot of pleasure, but they were not interested in how the real countryfolk lived. On their picnics they stayed away from the hovels of the peasants.

For these peasants the life in the towns and in the country châteaux seemed like something in a fairy tale, and out of their reach for ever. A visiting townsman or nobleman seemed a superior being to them, and the mail-coach passing on its way was like a messenger from another world. But it was their work and the taxes they paid that kept the country going.

This worried thoughtful men, for they saw the gap getting wider between the people in the towns and the people in the country. The ideas of these thinkers seem obvious to us but they were new and shocking in those days. They realised that man's work will be well done only if his pay is in proportion to the trouble he takes. Master and servant must show consideration for each other. A man was not a good servant if he felt he was looked down on, or was not allowed his pride or independence. And a man couldn't be a good boss if he imagined it was his high birth alone that gave him a right to authority and respect. So the peasants of France rose up against their rulers, who had treated them so badly.

UP TO 150 YEARS AGO

Big changes had taken place all over the world. The people of the British Colonies in North America had made themselves independent and had set up the United States of America. More and more new states were added until the U.S.A. became the great power that it is today. Then the Spanish and Portuguese colonies in America also made themselves free, though they remained as separate countries.

In France the people had rebelled against their king and his government because the country had been led into poverty and oppression by them. The king was imprisoned and then his head was cut off. He was not a bad man, but he was weak and unsuited for the job of running a great nation. The idea now was that the people should rule themselves, but they found out that self-government is a difficult affair. Before long the people found they had got a new set of rulers. Some of these were very able men, but others were dangerous. Napoleon was both able and dangerous. He turned the French republic into an empire, and won amazing victories for his country. He was a tremendous organiser, but quite ruthless. In the end he was defeated and he ended his life as a prisoner on the island of St Helena in the South Atlantic. France was poor and exhausted by then, and all Napoleon left to Europe, which he wanted to conquer, were some good roads, a collection (or 'Code') of laws and some palaces in a new style. This style was severe and straight, with every-

thing imitating the plain, sharp lines of ancient Greek temples. The fashion was named after Napoleon: the Empire style.

While Napoleon was disturbing the whole of Europe with his armies—and even before he had started—there were a number of events taking place which seemed strange, or even dangerous to the people of those times. We realize now that we have gained from these inventions. In Paris there was a man who went up in a balloon full of gas. In England an engine that was driven by steam had been invented. There was talk of using it to move ships through the water! A Dutch chemist had tried out a lamp fed by coal gas. A German forest-warden fixed two wheels, one behind the other, in a wooden frame, and dashed along the roads on it. The police disapproved, and banned the machine.

There were many other novelties, which aroused less excitement in public. In England the Spinning Jenny was invented by Hargreaves to make work easier for his wife, but the other workmen were so frightened of losing their jobs that they destroyed his machinery. A country clergyman called Cartwright perfected the power-loom, and in France a silk-weaver called Jacquard constructed a loom to weave all possible patterns, even the most complicated ones. A Swiss chemist living in Berlin found out how to get sugar from beets, and set up the first sugar-beet factory. Dr Jenner in his English country practice discovered how to vaccinate people against smallpox, and so defeated a plague that was killing more than 100,000 people every year in Europe. This was a much bigger and more important victory than was ever won by a general on a battlefield.

UP TO 100 YEARS AGO

At last we have two pages without mentioning wars. That doesn't mean there were no wars any more. In fact there were quite a lot of them, but other things that were happening were much more important. A hundred or more years ago the magic word was 'railways'. Right at the beginning when Stephenson ran the world's first steam train along the 38 miles of track from Stockton to Darlington, people were still very doubtful about the benefit of such a means of transport. Was a human being able to stand up to the fantastic speed of travelling at over 25 miles an hour? And what happened if a cow got onto the track? And wasn't the whole thing far too expensive? The mockers and doubters gradually became silent and soon pretended they had been in favour of railways all along. The tracks were being laid all over the land and there was a great

boom for those who had money to put into the railway companies. The lines spread faster than anybody expected. In Britain there were 2000 miles of them in 1844, nearly 7000 miles in 1850, and over 10,000 miles in 1860! On the continent and in America railways grew at the same pace. This was all due to the steam engine. Factory machines were being driven by steam and with plenty of coal dug up cheaply to feed the furnaces, industry was expanding tremendously.

So many things were happening so fast that it would need a whole book to include them all. Scientists were at work everywhere experimenting with electricity. People had known about it for a long time, but had only used it in parlour tricks. These experiments were the origin of the whole of electric power. The telegraph and telephone were only possible with the discovery of the

use of electricity. The scientists still had not quite succeeded in making electric lighting, but they went on trying with determination.

Another magic word of a hundred years ago was 'photography'. There had been the old *Camera Obscura*, but if needed the invention of two Frenchmen, Nièpce and Daguerre, to find a way of fixing pictures of people, places and things as negatives on plates. Fox Talbot made the next big step by inventing the first print negatives. From then on, photography progressed fast, and more and more people earned their living from their skill in taking pictures. Monsieur de Silhouette would have been surprised if he could have seen how cheaply we can take snapshots of one another!

Photographers regarded themselves almost as artists in those days. They sported floppy ties and fancy beards, and this dashing get-up was supposed to express what specially sensitive natures they had. Some of the early portrait photographs really were masterpieces, like one or two of those taken by Lewis Carroll, who wrote 'Alice in Wonderland'.

On the whole, the faces we see in the old photographs do not display much liveliness on the part of the sitters. Men and women looked very solemn indeed. The reason for this was that they had to sit like statues for so long, as the exposures took much more time than with our modern fast films. Just try sitting without moving for two minutes, with the same expression on your face!

What other things that we take for granted today were comparative novelties a hundred years ago? Postage stamps, matches, sewing machines, steel nibs, typewriters, petrol and concrete are just a few.

123

THE BEGINNING OF THIS CENTURY

The world was already looking very much as it does today, though some details, such as people's clothes, now look strange to us. But just how odd will our own clothes seem fifty years from now? The man going for a walk at the right of the picture seemed daring and comical in his day. We would simply say he must be feeling the heat.

The happy young couple off to the country on a tandem bicycle made everybody stare when these machines were new. Soon they became quite normal, and nowadays we can often see people riding them. The whole business of looking funny is not really important. You can scoff at whatever you like, but others have just as much right

to laugh at you if they feel there's something funny about you too.

At this period the magic word was 'motorcar'. This invention was originally called a horseless carriage, and the earliest models looked like it. They were just ordinary oldfashioned carriages with a motor built in somewhere. The first car with a petrol motor was built in 1875 by Marcus in Vienna. It was most unpopular with all other roadusers, and the police had to forbid it because the noise the machine made annoyed the other citizens.

The American name is 'automobile', a mixture of Greek and Latin words, meaning self-moving. This name is a link between the

modern and the ancient. Another link is the way in which we measure the power of a motor-car engine. It is called horse-power. This name is therefore a sort of permanent memorial to the horses which for so much of human history did the pulling and carrying for men. That is a rather nice thought to remember.

The motor car is sometimes said to have transformed our lives completely. Perhaps that is true, but it is just as true to say the same of all other modern inventions, even the safety match. Mankind's life is really changing all the time very slowly. The cause is never a single thing but all that has, over a long period of time, added to our comfort and increased our enjoyment of life. We are also being changed by our inventions that

do us harm as much as by ones that do us good. Some new things make a big stir, like the latest cars, others appear quietly, like the Braille script for the blind, or the ophthalmoscope for examining inside the eye, or the tiny jewel-stones that make watches accurate. Every one of them was like a revolution, just the same.

This century has included the two worst wars in history. They certainly showed that improvements in human nature have not gone very deep yet. As always before, these two wars were due to power-seeking, heart-lessness, revenge for past injuries, and pride.

One wonders whether people have become any happier nowadays. What do you think is the most important thing to make people happy?

Columbus's first fleet
Santa Maria · 100 tons · 52 men

Pinta · 50 tons · 18 men

Niña · 40 tons · 18 men

THE EXPLORERS

The great adventure of overseas discovery began when Columbus made his voyage in 1492. He was aiming to open the sea route to Zipangu, as Japan was then known, and to the rich shores of India and was convinced that he could sail westward round the world. He had no doubt that it was shaped like a ball. After a voyage of ten weeks he reached a little island in the Bahamas (Watling Island) which he named San Salvador. He made three other expeditions and several times touched the mainland of Central and South America. Seafarers of many nations were discovering other ocean routes, Cabot, a Genoese like Colombus, reached Newfoundland in 1497. Vasco da Gama found the real sea way to India round the Cape of Good Hope in 1498, and in 1519 another Portuguese, Magellan, set out with a Spanish fleet to sail right round the globe. Sir Francis Drake was the first Englishman to sail round the world. He left England in 1577 and returned in 1580. The opening up of the new continents lasted another 300 years. The Spanish and Portuguese explored South America. The English, Dutch and French went to North America. The Dutchman Tasman reached Australia, and Captain Cook charted the Pacific Ocean.

ASIA

The first European to travel in Central Asia was the Italian friar Carpini in 1246. The next one was the Flemish friar Rubroeck in 1253. The fullest and best account of travel in Asia was given by Marco Polo of Venice. With his father Nicolo and uncle Maffeo, he spent 26 years in the empire of Kublai Khan.

126

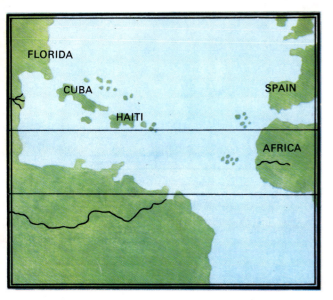

The navigators of 1513 drew the map of the Atlantic Ocean

East Indiaman about 1650

Captain Cook's Endeavour, 1768

AFRICA

Much of the coastline of the "Dark Continent" had been known for centuries, but the exploration of the interior only started with the founding of the African Association in London in 1788. It was after 1850 that most work was done. The greatest among the explorers were Mungo Park, Livingstone and Stanley.

THE POLAR REGIONS

The ice caps of the Arctic and Antarctic were the last blanks on the map. They were explored without the hope of finding riches there, and the courageous polar explorers did not guess their discoveries would become valuable for air routes. Peary reached the North Pole in 1909, and Amundsen the South Pole in 1911.

THE DISCOVERERS

Hammer and axe, spear, flint knife and bone needle—these were the first tools to be discovered and used by man more than 10,000 years ago. Wheels, boats, rudders, sails and the wooden plough have been known for perhaps 6,000 years. There are old legends which tell of these discoveries; in ancient times stories were never written down, only passed on by word of mouth. By the time the Greeks were building their beautiful temples, man had learnt how to smelt and cast metal expertly, to make artistic, decorated pottery vessels and glass; to understand the weaver's loom, the principles of the sundial and the water wheel.

PAPER PRINTING

Paper from the pith of the Papyrus reed:

	Egypt	c. 3000 BC
Parchment from skins		c. 1400 BC
Linen paper	China	c. 1300 BC
Rag paper	Italy	c. 1250 AD
Wooden stamp printing	China	c. 600 AD
Wooden moveable type	China	c. 1050 AD
Metal moveable type	Korea	c. 1400 AD
Gutenberg	Germany	1445 AD

OPTICS

Ground glass lenses:	Italy	c. 1250
Spectacles: (also compass and other astronomical instruments)	Italy	c. 1300
Microscope:		
Janssen Brothers,	Holland	1590
Hooke,	England	1665
Telescope: Lippershey,	Holland	1608
Improved by Galileo	Italy	1610
Prismatic telescope: Newton,	England	1669

CLOCKS

Clock driven by cogwheels in metal and wood, with weights, spring mechanism and escapement:

Germany and Switzerland   *c.* 1320

Pocket watch with spring balance:

Henlein, Germany   1509

Pendulum clock: Huygens, Holland   1657

Chronometer: Harrison, England   1735

SUCTION PUMPS

Suction and Vacuum pump:

Guericke, Germany   1663

Geuricke also experimented with frictional electricity and built an electrically-driven machine.

CHINA

In China   *c.* 600

In Europe   Tschirnhaus,
Böttger,
Germany   1693

LIGHTNING CONDUCTOR

Franklin, America   1752

STEAM ENGINE

First experiments: Papin, France   1690

Savery, Newcomen, England   *c.* 1710

First working steam engine:

Watt, England   1765

High compression steam engine
Trevithick, England   1803

STEAM SHIP

First experiments: Papin, France   1707

Jouffroy, France   1776

Symington, England   1786

Paddle steamer: Fulton, U.S.A.   1807

Ship's propellor: Ressel, Austria   1826

Propellor-driven steamship Archimedes:
Pettit-Smith, England   1836

RAILWAY

First experiments: Trevithick, Eng.   1803

Steam locomotive: Stephenson, Eng.   1829

First railroad: Stephenson, Eng.   1830

HOT AIR BALLOON AIRSHIP

Hot air balloon: Mongolfier, France   1783
Hydrogen balloon: Charles, France   1783
Airship with hydrogen:
     Renard and Krebs, Germany   1884
Graf Zeppelin airship, Germany   1900

BICYCLE

Drais, Germany   1817
(First bicycle factory
Michaux, France 1868)

MATCHES

Sulphur matches:
Jones, England   1822
   Phosphor matches:
   Kammerer, Germany
           1833

SEWING MACHINE

Saint, England   1790
Madersperger,
     Austria   1830
Hunt and Howe,
     England   1834

PHOTOGRAPHY

Niepce, France   1822
Daguerre, France   1838
Photographic paper
Fox Talbot,
England   1841

TELEGRAPHY

First experiments:
Lesage, France
Sommering, Gauss,
Weber, Germany
Wheatstone, Eng.
First electromag-
netic recording
telegraph:
   Morse, USA 1837

PETROLEUM

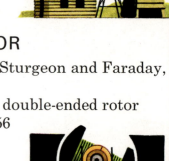

First oil well bored:
Drake, USA   1859

ELECTRIC MOTOR

Early experiments: Sturgeon and Faraday,
England
Electric motor with double-ended rotor
Siemens, Ger.   1856
Coiled armature
motor, Gramme
England   1869
Moving coil motor
Tesla, Austria   1887
Dynamo motor
Siemens, Ger.   1866

TYPEWRITER

Mitterhofer,
Austria   1864
Glidden and Scholes,
USA   1867

TELEPHONE

Early experiments:
Bourseul, France;
Meucci, Cuba; Reis,
Germany
First working tele-
phone:
Bell, USA   1877

EXPLOSIVES

Nitroglycerine:
Sobrero, France   1847
Nitrocellulose:
Schönbein,
Germany   1846
Dynamite: Nobel,
Sweden   1867

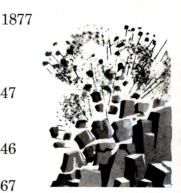

GRAMOPHONE

Edison, USA   1877
Record player:
Berliner, USA   1887
Magnetophone:
Poulsen,
Denmark   1898

ELECTRIC LIGHT

Goebel, USA   1854
Edison, USA   1879
Tungsten filament lamp:
Longmuir, USA   1913

MOTOR CAR

First petrol engine: Otto, Germany   1867
Petrol-driven automobile: Marcus,
      Austria   1875
         Benz and Daimler, Germany   1886
(First car factory: Daimler, Germany 1890)

CINEMATOGRAPHY

Lumiere Brothers,
France   1895
First film presentation:
Pathe, France   1895
Mester, Germany   1896
Sound film:
Vogt, Engl, Massolle,
Germany   1923

AIRCRAFT

First Glider flight: Lilienthal,
Germany   1891

First motorized flight: Wright brothers,
USA   1903
Gyroplane: La Cierva, Spain   1922
Jet engine: Schmidt, Germany   1930

X-RAYS

Röntgen, Germany 1895

WIRELESS TELEGRAPHY

Faraday, Maxwell,
Hertz, Brandly
Marconi, Italy 1897
Aerial circuit:
Popov, Russia 1900
Radio valves:
Meissner,
Germany   1913
First regular trans-
missions,
Germany   1921

TELEVISION

First scanner:
Nipkow, Russia 1884
Thermionic amplifier:
De Forest   1907
First successful
transmissions:
J. L. Baird UK; C. F.
Jenkins USA early
1920's

HELICOPTER

Sikorski, USA   1925

SYNTHETIC FIBRES

Artificial silk: Chardonnet, France   1884
Perlon: Schlack, Germany   1938
Nylon: Carothers, USA   1938

ATOMIC ENERGY

Early experiments: Rutherford, England;
Joliot-Curie, France; Hahn, Germany;
Meitner, Austria
First nuclear reactor: Fermi, USA   1942
Atomic-powered engine   1953
First power station: Calder Hall   1956

THE DEVELOPMENT OF TRANSPORT

Viking Ship Greek sailing ship Egyptian cargo boat

When you want to go on a journey all you have to do is to look at a timetable and buy a ticket. When you want to send something away you take it to the post or a transport firm. But at the beginning of the last century parcels and letters were sent by coach or carrier's cart and people travelled on horseback or in carriages. Only so short a time ago there were no railways or airlines and few shipping lines. And there were no travel agencies. The first was founded by Thomas Cook in 1845.

Travelling coach of the year 1500 Travelling coach of the year 1830

Examples of early American and European cars

Cadillac 1902

Ford 1909

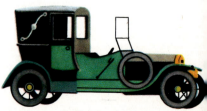

Rolls Royce 1915

Left, the screw of an early propeller steamer. Right, a more up-to-date model. Early steamers usually carried masts and sails in order to save coal when the wind was favourable

Zeppelin of the year 1909. The machine in which Bleriot flew across the Channel in 1909. Left, the English screw steamer *Archimedes* of the year 1836. The first steamers could not travel at nearly the speed of the great sailing ships, the fastest of which travelled from Japan to England with a cargo of tea in 99 days

Railway train of the year 1840

Daimler 1920   Lancia 1921   Oldsmobile 1931

133

INDUSTRIALIZATION

Industrialization means the extraction of raw materials from the earth, and the production of goods from those raw materials after they have been through the factories.

There is a great and important distinction between industrialization and the making of goods by hand. Things are made by hand one at a time, whereas industry provides a stock of goods for people to buy. A man in need of a suit, for instance, can go to his tailor, where he chooses the material and the tailor takes his measurements. The suit is then made specially for him. But the man can also go to a shop and buy a ready-made suit. The shop has a whole supply of suits which were made in an industrialized clothing factory.

It used not to be possible to take a boat up the river which runs through the industrial area shown in this picture. The current was too fast and the water was not deep enough. After the water level had been controlled by means of dams, boats were able to pass over these dams by means of locks. A barge is just about to enter the lock. The lower gate is open, the upper one shut. As soon as the barge is inside the lock the lower gate will be shut and the upper one opened. The water level will rise and the barge will be able to proceed up the river.

In some places industry has spread so much that there is hardly any unspoilt country left. Wherever you look in such districts you can see tall factory chimneys stretching away into the distance. Most of

High tension cables   Coal heap   Goods train

these factories have sprung up during the past hundred years, since what was called the "Industrial Revolution".

Since the invention of the steam engine and the electric motor nothing has been able to stop the growth of industry. Hordes of salesmen are busy everywhere, even in the smallest village, marketing the goods made in the factories. You might suppose that more and more factories are being built because people are continually needing fresh supplies of the things they produce. But many of the factories produce things which used not to exist at all, like cookers, television sets and electric fires. vision sets and electric fires.

More factories are also needed because there are more people in the world. In spite of war and starvation there are twice as many people in Europe as there were a hundred years ago and in America there are six times as many. It is clear that if everything were made by hand it would be impossible to provide people with all they needed, unless of course nearly everybody was working to make things by hand. But then there would not be enough people left to work at other things such as teaching, writing, painting, acting or dentistry.

There are so many branches of modern industry, often so closely connected, that it is not easy to explain them. First you must

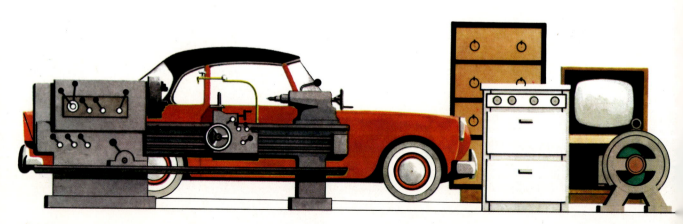

Chemicals factory   Water-tower   Oil tanks   Oil-well tower   Oil pump

understand that there are several great groups of industry which are dependent on each other. No single one of them can exist without the others. Mining works, foundries, iron and steel works, power stations, oil wells, paper factories, lime and cement works and chemical factories all produce raw materials which are used in other factories to make such things as machines, motor cars and bicycles, ships, tools, electrical and optical apparatus and delicate instruments. The factory itself cannot be built without materials which are made by yet other factories: bricks, tiles, flooring, door and window frames, insulating material and many other things. And the factory workers need many things for themselves and their families which are made in other factories: clothes, shoes, furniture, pots and pans, books, newspapers, musical instruments and toys. And when the workers go home they use other things which other factories have produced for them: bread, milk and sugar, beer and wine, sausages, chocolate, noodles and preparations such as pudding mixtures and soup cubes.

It is all very complicated and confusing. And in order to get what he wants, whether it be a new car or a glass of milk, a man must pay for it with the money he earns at work. On the next page you will find out more about how we pay for things.

NUMBERS

When the Arabs crossed the Mediterranean to Spain more than a thousand years ago they brought with them something which until then was unknown in Europe. It was small and round. It represented nothing and it was very important. It was the figure 0.

The Arabs didn't invent it. They probably got it from the Chinese and perhaps from India—nobody knows for certain. We ought all to be very pleased that we have a nought even if it does mean nothing. If you write down a whole row of noughts underneath the figure one, when you add the sum up the number remains the same. But put the nought after the figure one and you get ten; two noughts gives one hundred; three noughts gives one thousand.

Without the figure nought we should still have to do our sums in the same way as the ancient Romans and we know that they had great difficulty in doing sums. Great progress was made in mathematics as soon as the Arabic figures came into use. The very word *algebra* is an Arabic word.

It is clear that it matters very much where you put the nought. And this is true of all the other figures too. This is the whole secret of the Arabic method of counting, which seems so simple and yet which can be so puzzling.

The first and chief use of the figure nought is to make the number ten. Before the invention of numbers people could only count as far as ten and then they had to start all over again. They counted on their fingers and sometimes they also used pebbles, shells and fruit stones to help them to add up. They counted long before they learned to read and write. Another way of counting is with an abacus, which has beads strung on wires, ten at a time.

THE ROMAN NUMERALS

You can often see Roman numerals on clock faces, in books to number the chapters and on old monuments. The Romans used seven letters to make up their numbers: I for 1, V for 5, X for 10, L for 50, C for 100, D for 500 and M for 1000. All the other numbers they got by adding and subtracting. For instance IV means 4— that is one *less* than 5, whereas VI means 6—one *more* than 5 and so on all through. Here are some numbers:

I	II	III	IV	V	VI	VII	VIII	IX	X	XI	XII
1	2	3	4	5	6	7	8	9	10	11	12

XIX	XX	XXX	XL	L	LX	XC	C
19	20	30	40	50	60	90	100

CC	CD	D	DC	CM	M	MM
200	400	500	600	900	1000	2000

To make dates you must add the letters up like this:

```
1975  =  1000 =  M
      plus  500 =      D
      plus  400 =          CCCC
      plus   50 =              L
      plus   20 =                  XX
      plus    4 =                      IV
      ————  =  ————————————————
      1974 =  MDCCCCLXXIV
```

MONEY

Early trading was all done by a system of exchange, but this was very clumsy so people decided to use precious metals such as copper, silver and gold, the worth of which was known to everyone, to indicate the value of goods. The metal was not made into coins but was kept in lumps of various weights which were exchanged for goods. But this was too complicated so at last money was invented, probably by the Persians. It consisted of small round discs of a definite weight and stamped with a particular design so that everyone could be sure they were genuine. Money was so practical that more and more trading peoples began to issue coins of their own— stamped with a portrait of their king or with an emblem of their country.

But the invention of money did not make things much easier for very rich people. When they went on a journey they were weighed down by heavy bags of money or they carried precious stones which they had to sell to pay for their needs. And they went in constant fear of robbers.

The Italians were the first to think of a way out of this difficulty. Rich men left their money in the hands of certain great merchants, who gave them in return pieces of paper saying how much money there was. So paper money was born—much handier and less bulky than coins, although coins were still useful for small change. In addition, a rich man could go on his travels, and if he wanted to buy something in another town he could send a letter to his "banker" ordering him to pay the price to the seller. These letters were the first cheques.

Netherlands   France   Gt. Britain   Spain   Belgium

Canada   Eire   Germany   Guernsey   U.S.A.

THE EARTH

THE GLOBE

When people first discovered that the earth was round they immediately wanted to know what all the other sides of the globe looked like. It was tremendous task to find out and it was a long time before all the blank areas on the map—the parts which had not yet been explored—were filled in. But even the tiniest, most distant islands have now been discovered and named. All the sea coasts have been explored and marked on the map. The vast deserts have all been surveyed; and places where no human being has ever set foot have been examined from the air.

In order to understand exactly what the earth looks like it is necessary to use a globe. This shows the correct positions of the different countries and seas, especially in the regions near the north and south poles. If you were looking at a flat map Greenland and Siberia would appear to lie very far apart. In reality, as you can see at once from the globe, they are much closer to each other than are Africa and South America.

It is interesting to know how the different continents got their names. Asia, the largest continent, is called after a meadow, the Asian field near Ephesus in present-day Turkey. The Greeks gave the name Asia to the country which lay to the east of their islands. Later the name was used for Persia as well and finally it was given to all the vast territory which is known as Asia today.

Africa was given its name by the Romans. The word comes from *Africani*, the name of a people who lived on the north coast of the continent in the time of the Romans.

The word America was first used by a map maker who lived by Lake Constance. He had to draw a map illustrating the journeys of an Italian called Amerigo Vespucci and as he was not sure what name to write on the map

NORTH AMERICA

EUROPE

ASIA

AFRICA

The Equator

SOUTH AMERICA

AUSTRALASIA

ANTARCTICA

red   white   black   yellow   brown

he wrote the name of the Italian explorer.

The part of the world in which the South Pole lies is called the Antarctic which means 'the opposite of the Arctic' and the Arctic is where the North Pole is to be found. The name comes from the Greek word *arktos* which means '*bear*'. The Great Bear and the Little Bear are the names of constellations or groups of stars which shine in the north.

Europe gets its name from Europa, a king's daughter who, according to the Greek legend, was carried off by the god Zeus.

Australia is the smallest of the continents. It was given its name "terra australis" or southern land by a Spaniard, Quiros, a courageous cavalier who made many journeys across the Pacific in search of the new continent. He never got there but the Dutch later adopted Quiros' idea.

The people who inhabit the various parts of the globe are differently coloured. Their skin may be white, black, yellow, brown or copper. Europeans, their descendants and many of the people of western Asia are white. African negroes and their descendants, and the original inhabitants of Australia, are black. The people of eastern Asia, the Japanese, Chinese and Mongolians, are yellow. The people from southern Asia and many of the islands of the Pacific are brown, though a few of the latter are black; and American Indians are copper-coloured.

The distinctions are not so clear as they once were. In former times people generally lived all their lives in their own country, but nowadays men of different colour are living together nearly everywhere.

143

The Himalayas, the highest mountains in the world

A blossoming spray from a tea plant

ASIA

More than half the people of the whole world live in Asia. Many clever men were born there and many of the inventions and ideas which in the course of time have spread all over the world came first from Asia. The numbers by which you count came from India. Paper and porcelain and also the compass were invented in China. In far-off times merchants used to bring back wonderful materials from China, finer than anything which had ever been seen in Europe. In Rome, 2,000 years ago, silk was literally worth its weight in gold. The Chinese kept the secrets of their silk manufacture very carefully, but about 1500 years ago two Persian monks who lived in China managed to smuggle some silkworms' eggs out to Constantinople, after which silk manufacture spread throughout the Middle East and Europe. Many other things, food and raw materials, come from Asia: tea and rice, cane sugar, spices, dyes, petroleum and also remedies such as opium and camphor.

THE SILKWORM

There is a certain moth which can live only where there are mulberry trees. The caterpillars which hatch from this moth's eggs feed on mulberry leaves for several weeks, growing fat and round. Then, from their glands, they spin a fine thread in which they wrap themselves round and round forming a cocoon. These spun sheaths are about the size of small plums. It is from their threads that real Chinese silk is woven.

An elk, a bear and a wolf from Siberia

A Bactrian camel and a yak from Central Asia

An Indian elephant with a baby, and a zebu

A sportsman had to spend a night in the jungle, so he took a goat with him. He tied it to a tree nearby. "If a tiger comes," he thought, "it will attack the goat, and its cries will wake me up." Late at night a tiger approached. The sportsman was fast asleep, and the poor goat shook with fright. But the tiger had never seen a goat before. "What a courageous beast", it thought, "that doesn't run off at the sight of me." So the tiger slunk away.

In Northern China is found the world's largest work built by man—the great wall of China. If it were laid on the map of Europe, it would run from Calais to Constantinople—1500 miles. It was begun over 2000 years ago to protect China from the fierce raiders on horseback from Mongolia, but it was never properly finished. It did not really protect China from invasions. Now much of it has been pulled down.

A baby orang-utang and its parent, from Sumatra

Proboscis monkey (Borneo)   Gibbon (Siam)   Langur from India

It is possible to get a crop of rice three times a year in the hot parts of Asia and in the islands to the south-east. Rice also grows in China, Japan and Korea. It needs a lot of sunshine, but even more important, a lot of water. The fields are called paddies and look like swamps, as they have to be kept flooded. Cultivating rice is hard work, and the seedlings need re-planting by hand several times under the water. All this is worthwhile because rice is such a nourishing food. Rice flour is also used to make glue, starch and make-up powders. The straw is useful for matting, too.

IRAN

The buildings where the Muslims go to pray in the Arab countries, and in Turkey, Iran and Pakistan, are called mosques. They have a big courtyard and a building with a dome on top. The walls are richly decorated with wonderful patterns, often on coloured tiles, and these patterns have been imitated all over the world on materials such as Paisley shawls and on carpets. The onion-shaped domes, with the tall minarets close by—they are towers with a balcony from which the people are called to prayer at regular times every day—also inspire other buildings in many countries.

BAMBOO

This grows in all the tropical parts of Asia. Bamboo is really a giant kind of grass which shoots up very quickly, even reaching 120 feet—higher than the trees! The young shoots are a delicious vegetable, and the hard, shiny stems are used for many things people need: baskets, ladders, fences, carts, houses and bridges. Old stems are strong enough to be used for making cooking pots.

JAPAN

The Japanese have no beds in their unusual and attractive houses. Instead, mats and blankets are taken out of the built-in cupboards at night and rolled out on the splotless floor. The Japanese are very clean and tidy and leave their shoes or sandals at the front door when they come in. The houses are lightly built of wood, with partitions made of matting or thin plaster. The windows still usually have oiled paper instead of panes of glass.

CHINA

The German monk Berthold Schwartz or the English scholar Roger Bacon may have been the first to invent gunpowder 700 years ago, but the Chinese had something like it much earlier. But they never thought of using gunpowder for war and killing— not even for hunting! They preferred to add various minerals to the mixture of saltpetre, carbon and sulphur to produce sparkling coloured fireworks. All the religious festivals in China and Japan call for fire-crackers, and so do weddings. Without fireworks a celebration would seem very disappointing there. The Chinese have many poems on the subject and give different varieties pretty names, just as we do, like water rose, fire-wheel, diamond sun, magic bird, fountain, and waterfall.

BALI

Malaya and Indonesia are the home of the shadow-plays. They are found in all the villages. The figures are silhouettes cut out of hard cow-hide, with joints in the arms and legs, which are moved by long, thin rods from underneath. Their capering shadows are seen through a brightly lit screen. The adventures they act are quite like our own fairy tales and legends. A lovely princess is carried off by bad spirits just when she is going to be married. Her brother and the bridegroom have to set off in search of her and this takes them far and wide. They defeat dangerous ghosts, monsters, dragons and witches, and at last, helped by kindly spirits, they rescue the poor princess.

CANARY
ISLANDS

TANGIER

ALGIERS

TUNIS

TRIPOLI

A Moroccan

A Tuareg

Sudanese cameleer

CAIRO

Suez Canal

Pyramids at Giza

Nile

SAHARA

DAKAR

Niger

Balante

Straw hut with a palisade
against wild beasts

Mud house

Acacia

ADDIS ABABA

An Ethiopian

EQUATOR

ATLANTIC OCEAN

Congo

Baobab

A Watusi

A Thonga

Mozambique

Zambezi

MADAGASC

Straw-roofed mud hut

A Basuto

Decorated Zulu house

PRETORIA

CAPE TOWN

Elephant   Rhinoceros   Ostrich   Giraffe   Zebra   Springbok   Kudu

AFRICA

The African continent begins not very far away from us—just across the straits of Gibraltar. But it goes on a very long way further. Africa's size is so great that if a railway line ran all the way, linking Algiers with Cape Town, the trip would take an express train four whole days and nights. Perhaps a railway line like that will be built one day, but in any case, you can go everywhere in Africa by air. A steamer takes a whole month to complete the round trip by sea. If you decided to walk all the way to Cape Town, it would take you the best part of a year, and then only if you didn't slow down. And on the road south, you would first have to find your way across the Sahara, where there are no rivers and lakes, and it almost never rains. That part would take two months alone, if you survived. Not long ago, Africa was called the Dark Continent—not because the people there have black skins, but because so much of the interior was still unknown. Nowadays even remote African villages are in the world's daily news.

ELEPHANT STORIES

We call the lion the King of Beasts on account of its size, strength and fierce looks, and its loud roar. The Africans do not agree. They look on the elephant as the King of Beasts, as it is the largest living creature on the earth. The elephant is safe from all other animals which could not kill or even harm it. Men could manage to wound elephants with poisoned arrows or trap them, and take their valuable ivory tusks. But it is dangerous to attack those big feet and waving trunks! Only hunters with their rifles could easily slaughter the elephants. Nowadays people are not allowed to shoot elephants whenever they want to—they have to get a hunting licence. But elephants are still in danger from gangs of ivory poachers.

There are many marvellous stories about elephants and what they can do. Some of these things seemed impossible, but by now the naturalists have found out how much really is true about the elephants—and it is quite a lot.

Zulu warrior

Gorilla   Baboon   Hippopotamus   Crocodile   Marabou   Pelican   Lion

As an example, it used to be denied that elephants live to be one or two hundred years old. However, naturalists now think that some elephants may reach 250 years old. A lot of information comes from the big-game hunters, who are not always careful about the facts. What the natives themselves say about elephants cannot always be trusted either. They are afraid of elephants, and when people are afraid of something, they make it sound even bigger. But there is no doubt that there is still a great deal to be learned about these great animals. It is

true that elephants are clever. The Africans say they can even talk to each other. The explanation may be that elephants often doze with their heads together, and it looks as though one is whispering in its neighbour's ear. Elephants are supposed to have long memories. All we know for certain is that a wounded elephant is very dangerous because it remembers the scent of the humans who shot it. It will attack them furiously, long afterwards, or chase them for a long way across the country.

THE AFRICANS

White people have done many cruel things to the Africans. They used to capture Negroes and make them work in their plantations and mines for no money and little food. The whites thought the blacks were so inferior that they could be used like cattle, in order that the whites could get rich. Only a hundred years ago the slave-trade was still accepted as normal in the colonies of many countries. Slavery was officially ended in the British colonies in 1833 and in the U.S.A. in 1864.

However, the Africans do owe some good things to white people. Schools and teachers came to Africa with them, and many of the black people's old fears of bad spirits and powers have been eliminated. Hospitals and

An oasis or settlement around one of the few springs in the Sahara desert

doctors also came to Africa, to fight the terrible diseases spread by flies and worms and dirty water.

Many Africans are Christians now, but that does not mean that all the old customs have been given up. Old and new ideas are sometimes mingled. A Christian African man goes to his priest or pastor to get married, but he may go and consult a witch-doctor, too. He probably gives his wife's father six or eight oxen in exchange for his pretty daughter, just as marriage settlements and dowries are arranged in some Western countries.

The African thinks it is a good idea to keep on good terms with everybody—with the clergyman, the witch-doctor and his father-in-law. He may light a candle in the Catholic Mission Church and ask the saints to look after him, but at the same time he remembers his grandmother's tales of the souls of dead people going to live in the forests and sometimes coming out to visit their friends. The African will not work on Sunday, because that is the Christian rule, but he also refuses to do things on other special days—for example he never goes on a journey or builds a new hut when there is a new moon, because his old traditions say that this will bring bad luck. All people, all over the world, cling to some of their old customs and superstitions.

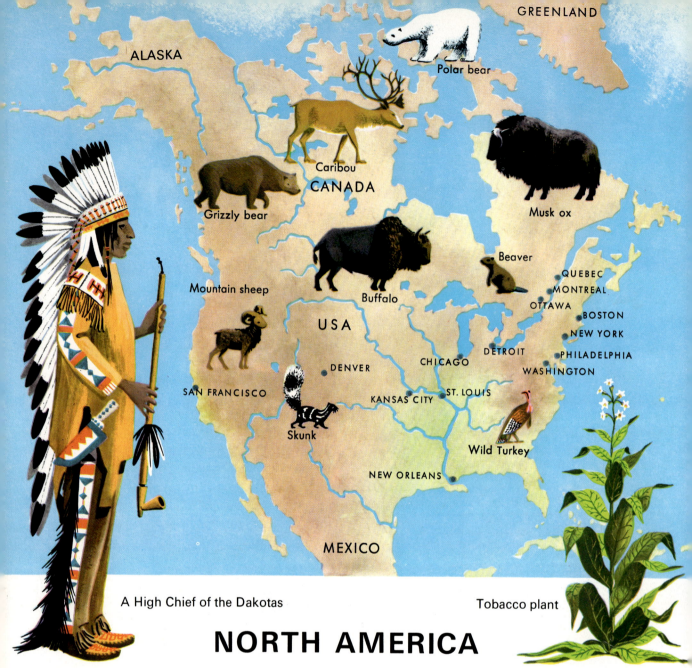

ALASKA

GREENLAND

Polar bear

Caribou

CANADA

Grizzly bear

Musk ox

Beaver

Buffalo

QUEBEC
MONTREAL
OTTAWA
BOSTON
NEW YORK
DETROIT
PHILADELPHIA
WASHINGTON

Mountain sheep

USA

DENVER

CHICAGO

SAN FRANCISCO

KANSAS CITY

ST. LOUIS

Skunk

Wild Turkey

NEW ORLEANS

MEXICO

A High Chief of the Dakotas

Tobacco plant

NORTH AMERICA

Until the Europeans arrived, the whole continent belonged to the Indians. Nobody knows how many of them there were, but they spoke about 150 different languages. We still use a few of their words for things not known before Columbus's time—tobacco, cigar, cocoa, chocolate, maize, tomato, potato.

Millions of people left Europe to find new homes in America, and descendants of all the nations go to make today's Americans. Here is what a settler wrote to his family a hundred years ago: "My new house is finer than any belonging to the richest neighbours at home, and my farmstead is as big as the fields of four of your villages put

together, and I want you all to come over and join me. The journey is difficult, but you will soon forget about it afterwards. For over here workdays are like your Sundays and we eat more meat than you eat bread, and we drink more coffee than you drink water. The buildings in our towns are as high as your church steeples, and in the fields the corn grows as high as the top of one's head. If I ever get homesick, I just remind myself of how well off I am here, and of the terrible poverty there was in the old country. You'll see it the same way too once you're over here. God grant it comes to pass." There must have been many letters like that.

New York harbour, in the biggest city of the USA

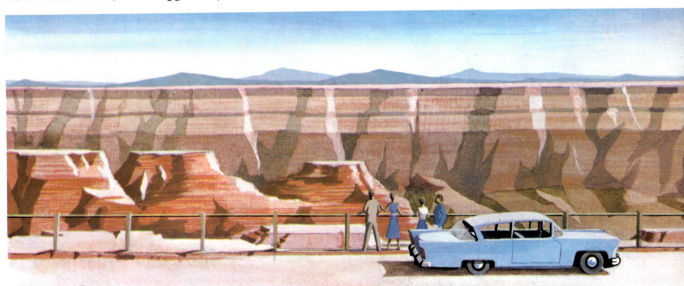

The Grand Canyon of the Colorado River, Arizona

Texan cowboys

THE WEST INDIES

The people of the West Indies are descended from captured Africans who were brought over to work as slaves in the plantations, but in spite of their sad history, the West Indians are cheerful and they enjoy dressing in gay costumes at carnival time and singing and playing. They have invented a new kind of music, called the 'steel band', where the players strike circular pieces of metal which look rather like large tin lids, and which give different notes when they are hit in different places. Many West Indian songs and melodies have become world-famous.

The West Indies were discovered by Columbus, who thought he had found India! The islands are very fertile and coffee, cocoa, coconuts, pineapples, lemons, bananas, spices and sugar are grown there. Sponges and pearls are found off the coasts of the Bahamas, where there are thousands of turtles and flamingoes.

Some of the West Indian islands are uninhabited, and they are just like the island on which Robinson Crusoe was shipwrecked. Now all the Caribbean islands are becoming very popular with people who want to have a holiday where the sun shines and everything is quite different from our busy, grey industrial towns. On the other hand, a lot of West Indians have crossed the sea to England to look for better and more interesting jobs.

Before they became independent, the islands did not all belong to the same nations; Haiti was French, and during the eighteenth century a negro called Toussaint led the people in revolt against the French. They lived as free men for seven years, but eventually Napoleon captured Toussaint and imprisoned him. Jamaica used to be a special haunt of smugglers and pirates and lawless men who had fled from Europe.

156

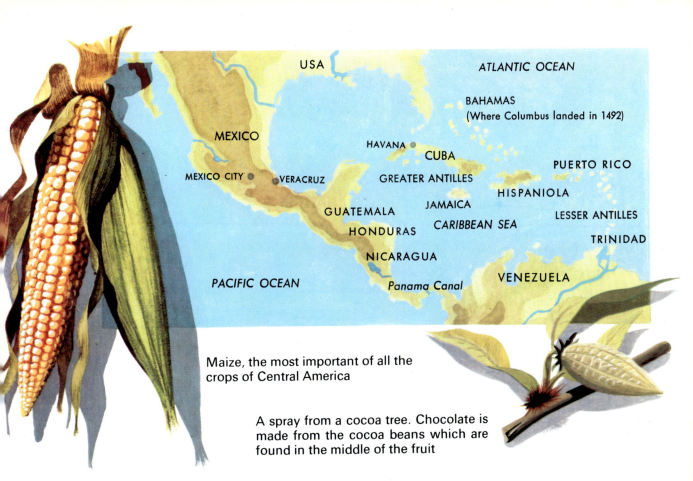

Maize, the most important of all the crops of Central America

A spray from a cocoa tree. Chocolate is made from the cocoa beans which are found in the middle of the fruit

MEXICO

Mexico is a country of mountains and great forests, tropical vegetation, lakes and marshes. The people are descended both from the Indians and from the Spanish conquerors. Maize, wheat, coffee and cotton are grown there as well as oranges, lemons, grapefruit, mangoes, bananas and other kinds of tropical fruit.

The earliest of the Indian groups were the Mayas; later came the Toltecs and finally the Aztecs, who built wonderful cities and temples which flourished from the 12th century until the Spanish conquest under Cortes in 1521. The Aztec city Tenochtitlàn was built on the same site as present-day Mexico City, the capital.

A Mexican Indian with a spray from a cotton plant. Half of all the world's cotton comes from the southern states of America and from Mexico

SOUTH AMERICA

The Panama Canal is where South America begins. Just as in North America, the original people living in South America were the Indians, but here they are still an important part of the population. The rest are descended from the Spanish and Portuguese who landed in about 1500 to conquer South and Central America. They wanted gold and jewels, but also they found a new home. Now there are busy cities and prosperous countries.

Much of South America is dense jungle or bleak mountains, but in the great modern cities around the coast life is the same as in Europe or the U.S.A. All the time progress is spreading to the interior.

Panama Canal

CARACAS

TRINIDAD

VENEZUELA

COLOMBIA

BOGOTA

Peruvian Indian feather embroidery

Indian pile-dwelling on the Amazon

BELEM

GALAPAGOS ISLANDS

PERU

LIMA

BRAZIL

RECIFE

Coral snake

BOLIVIA

LA PAZ

Amazonian Indians with bow and blow-pipe

SAO PAOLO

BRAZIL

RIO DE JANEIRO

Jaguar

SANTIAGO

CHILE

URUGUAY

MONTEVIDEO

BUENOS AIRES

ARGENTINA

Condor

The coffee bean originally grew in Africa, but the climate of Brazil, Colombia and Venezuela is so suitable for it that the world's biggest crops now come from there. The beans grow in pairs inside a red fruit that looks like a cherry

Two Chilean Indians travelling in the Andes mountains. The llamas are tame animals, a good deal bigger than sheep. They carry heavy loads and also give milk and wool. They are quite friendly, but spit if annoyed

IN THE JUNGLE

There are many varieties of toucan, all having big coloured beaks

The spider-monkey is able to walk, pick fruit and even wrestle with its tail

Some parrots are supposed to live to be 100

The sloth hangs for hours from a branch, doing nothing. Although it can climb well with its curved claws, it is helpless on the ground

A humming bird in the air. Some varieties are the size of butterflies and almost as light

These two creatures live on insects, the ant-eater (left) and the armadillo

The mangrove tree, the buttress tree and the rubber tree. Rubber is obtained by cutting the bark and letting the sap trickle out. It is then treated by heat to harden it

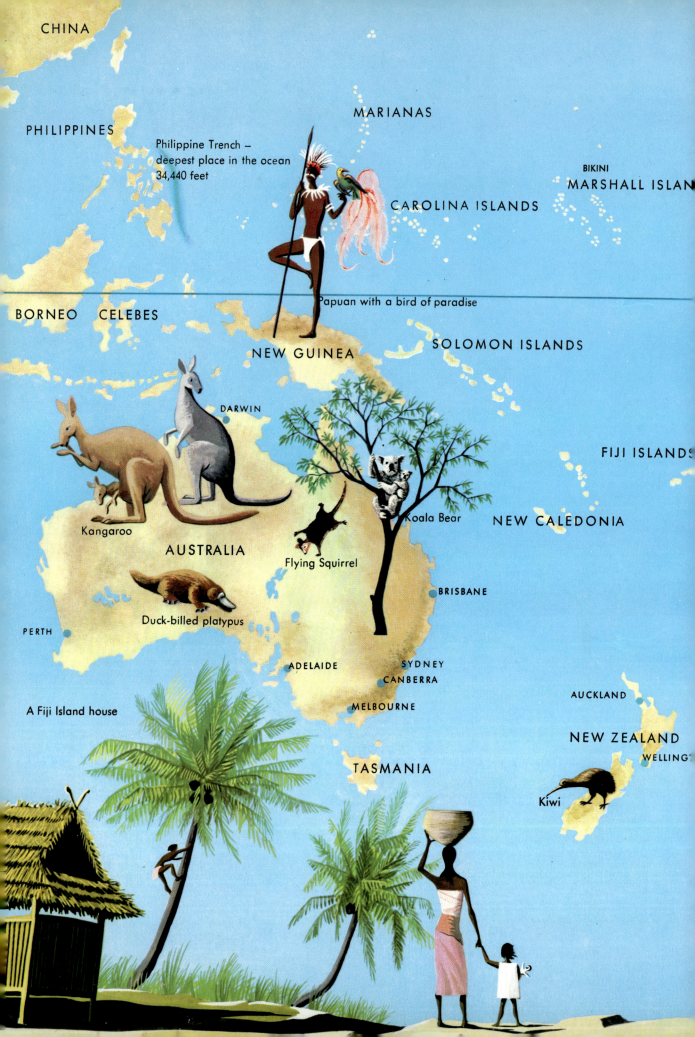

CHINA

PHILIPPINES

Philippine Trench —
deepest place in the ocean
34,440 feet

MARIANAS

BIKINI
MARSHALL ISLAN

CAROLINA ISLANDS

BORNEO   CELEBES

Papuan with a bird of paradise

NEW GUINEA

SOLOMON ISLANDS

FIJI ISLANDS

DARWIN

Kangaroo

AUSTRALIA

Flying Squirrel

Koala Bear

NEW CALEDONIA

Duck-billed platypus

PERTH

BRISBANE

A Fiji Island house

ADELAIDE

SYDNEY
CANBERRA

MELBOURNE

AUCKLAND

NEW ZEALAND

WELLING

TASMANIA

Kiwi

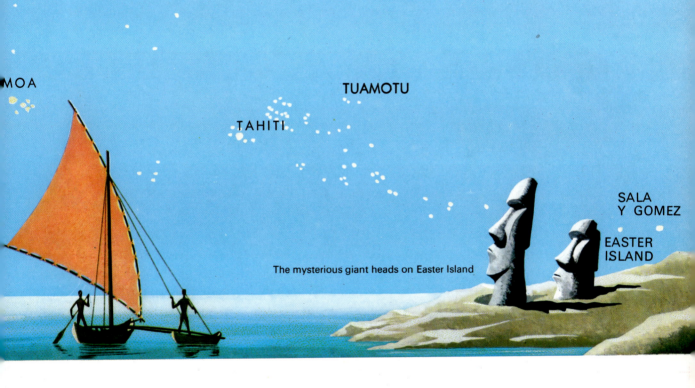

MIDWAY ISLANDS

MEXICO

WAKE
ISLAND

HONOLULU
HAWAIIAN ISLANDS

AUSTRALASIA

CHRISTMAS ISLAND

EQUATOR

MOA

TUAMOTU

TAHITI

The mysterious giant heads on Easter Island

SALA
Y GOMEZ

EASTER
ISLAND

The first Europeans to reach Australia were the Dutch. British settlements on the coast soon followed, and these have now grown to to be important cities. At first the distance from Europe was so great and the climate thought to be so harsh that few colonists went there. Now, however, people from all over Europe have emigrated to Australia, which has become a great and wealthy country with reserves of minerals and precious stones and a highly successful agricultural industry. Some of the native inhabitants of Australia, the aborigines, are still to be found there. Australia has some interesting animals of which the kangaroo is one. It has huge hind legs and with them can make powerful leaps at high speed, balancing itself with its thick tail. The mother-kangaroo carries her baby in a pouch of fur on her stomach. The koala bear mothers carry their babies in the same way. In New Zealand is found the Kiwi, a bird with poor wings and no tail, which cannot fly but runs very fast.

161

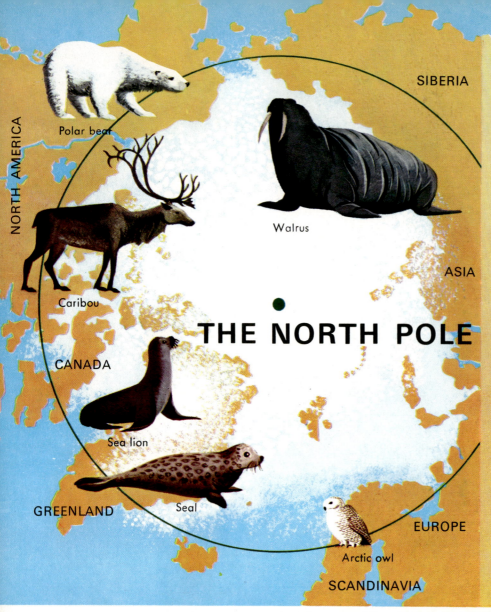

SIBERIA

NORTH AMERICA

Polar bear

Walrus

ASIA

Caribou

THE NORTH POLE

CANADA

Sea lion

GREENLAND

Seal

EUROPE

Arctic owl

SCANDINAVIA

The ancient Greek historian Herodotus heard a story in Asia that where the North Wind comes from there are people who sleep for half the year. The truth is that during the Arctic winter the sun does not rise over the horizon and the days are as dark as the nights. (Turn to page 167 if you wonder why!)

The North Pole is in the middle of an ocean that is frozen over with a thick layer of floating ice. Ships only sail round the edge in the summer, but submarines go right underneath. Few people live here unless, like fishermen and weather men, they have to, but for the Eskimos it is home.

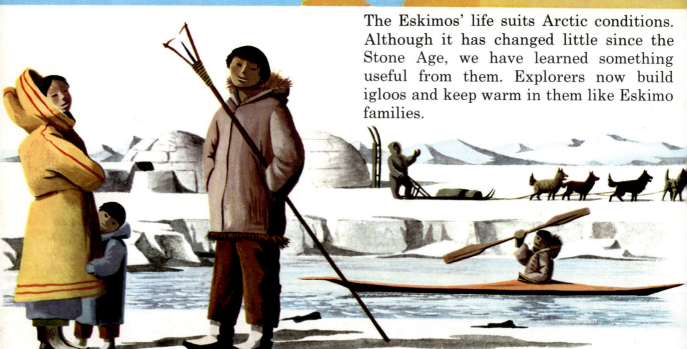

The Eskimos' life suits Arctic conditions. Although it has changed little since the Stone Age, we have learned something useful from them. Explorers now build igloos and keep warm in them like Eskimo families.

The kayak canoe and the anorak are Eskimo inventions, too

SOUTH AMERICA

GRAHAM LAND

The Antarctic is a solid continent of high mountains buried under ice which never melts. No plants grow anywhere, apart from some mosses at the end of Graham land, facing Cape Horn. The only living creatures apart from fishes are penguins and seals. Humans can only survive there if everything they need is supplied to them by ship or aircraft, but with this help some explorers have lived there in tunnel shelters for more than a year.

●

THE SOUTH POLE

ROSS ICE SHELF

MOUNT EREBUS (Volcano)

from Australia

Penguins are birds, but cannot fly. They swim, however, just as well as the seals do. They live in large flocks on the ice-cliffs and islands

A weather station in Antarctica

THE SKY

DAY AND NIGHT · SUN AND MOON

It takes the earth one year to travel round the sun and during that time it spins round 365 times. The only sign of this spinning which we can see is the movement of the sun in the sky as it travels from east to west. It seems to us that the earth is quite still. For that reason people used to think that the sun travelled round the earth. The astronomer Copernicus was the first to discover 450 years ago that this could not be true. He observed the movements of the other planets which seem to revolve in spirals. But if, instead of the earth, the sun is taken as the centre about which everything turns, then these spirals become circles. And the sun is indeed the central point. The time from midnight to midnight is one day, although we usually speak of the hours of light as 'day' and the hours of darkness as 'night'. All the light on the earth comes from the sun and without the sun there would be no life. The moon has no light of its own; it shines with light reflected from the sun. The journey which it *seems* to make round the earth takes a little longer than a day.

Looking at the earth from high above the North Pole
Daylight in Europe, Africa and Asia

Daylight in America

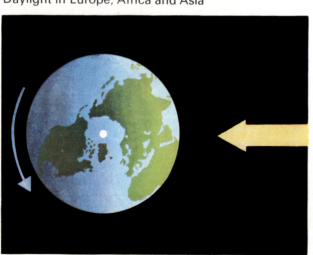

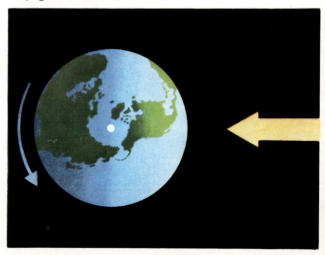

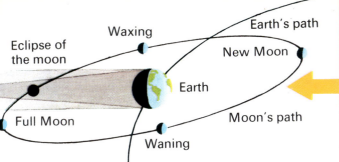

THE QUARTERS OF THE MOON

Sometimes we see the whole, or full, moon, sometimes only a part of it or one of the moon's quarters, and sometimes, though it is there in the sky, we cannot see it at all. Every 28 days (which is the time the moon *really* takes to circle the earth) it goes through these changes, because it reflects more or less of the sun's light to us as it moves round. After the new moon, the right side reflects more and more light until at last after 14 days it is completely full. Then the left side remains bright but shrinks night by night to a thin crescent until nothing is left.

When the moon is full its orbit may pass right through the shadow cast by the earth. The moon is then in eclipse and we lose sight of it for a few hours. When the moon is new it may pass between us and the sun, blocking the sun's light. This is an eclipse of the sun.

THE SEASONS

Twice a year on March 21st and September 23rd the axis of the earth is exactly perpendicular to its orbit round the sun. Between these times it leans, first one way, then the other. On June 21st the north pole is turned towards the sun and on December 22nd the south pole.

The yellow arrow on each of the three pictures on the right shows the direction from which the sun's rays are coming. The steeper they fall the warmer the weather. The top picture shows the position of the earth on June 21st. It is summer then in Europe, and round the North Pole the sun shines all night. The middle picture shows the position on March 21st (spring) and on September 23rd (autumn). In the bottom picture it is winter and cold in the North.

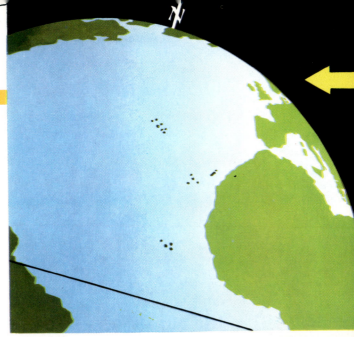

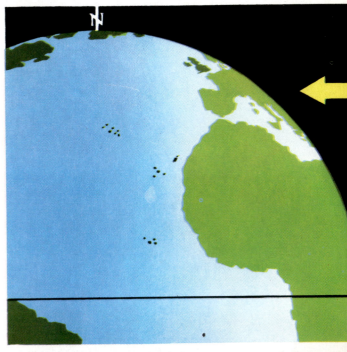

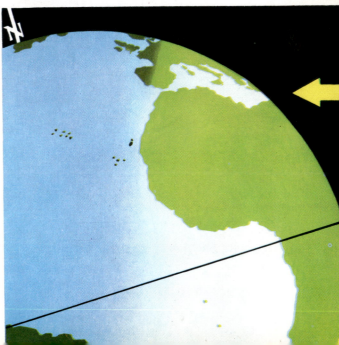

Path of a comet

THE PLANETS

Nine planets circle around the sun. One of these is the earth. The drawing at the top of this page shows their paths while on the left you can see their sizes in relation to each other. The great white disc on which this is written shows the enormous size of the sun—more than a hundred times the diameter of the earth.

MERCURY · Diameter 3,100 miles. Time taken to go round the sun, 88 days

VENUS · Diameter 7,700 miles. Time taken to go round the sun 225 days. At certain times of the year this is the brightest star in the sky

EARTH · Diameter 7,927 miles. Time taken to go round the sun 365 days. The moon is about one quarter the diameter of the earth

MARS · Diameter 4,220 miles. Time taken to go round the sun 687 days. It shines with a fiery red colour and has two very small moons

JUPITER · Diameter 88,770 miles. Time taken to go round the sun nearly twelve years. It is encircled by 12 moons

SATURN · Diameter 74,200 miles. Time taken to go round the sun 29 years. It is surrounded by a double ring of gas and accompanied by nine moons

- ♅ URANUS · Diameter 32,400 miles. Time taken to go round the sun 84 years. It has five moons

- ♆ NEPTUNE · Diameter 30,900 miles. Time taken to go round the sun 165 years. It has two moons

- ♇ PLUTO · Diameter 7,900 miles. Time taken to go round the sun 248 years

Thousands of small bodies known as planetoids are moving round the sun between the orbits of Mars and Jupiter. They are too small to be seen with the naked eye.

AURIGA · CASSIOPEIA · THE GREAT BEAR · THE POLE STAR · THE LITTLE BEAR · CEPHEUS · DRACO

THE FIXED STARS

The fixed stars are an immense distance away from us and from the sun. It takes the light from the nearest star four years to reach the earth. We call them fixed because their position in relation to one another never changes. They only seem to us to rise and set because the earth is going round. They vary greatly in size and brightness. The very smallest of them are as big as the earth. One of the largest, Antares, is over a hundred million times bigger than the sun.

There is one star which shines directly above the north pole and looks to us like the centre about which the stars are moving. This is the pole star by which for thousands of years sailors steered their courses. Round about it you can see some of the constellations of the northern hemisphere. There are other bodies in the sky besides stars: comets and meteors. Meteors are fragments, mostly small, which wander through space and burn up if they enter the earth's atmosphere. They are usually so small that nothing is left of them, but sometimes a residue falls to the earth in the form of meteorites. Meteors have never been known to cause any damage. Comets are made of gas and meteor-like fragments and travel in long-drawn-out paths. When they approach the sun they shine out brightly and leave a tail of fire behind them.

Below left, a telescope built in England by the astronomer Herschel. With this in 1781 he discovered Uranus and Saturn

Right, a small observatory with the dome open

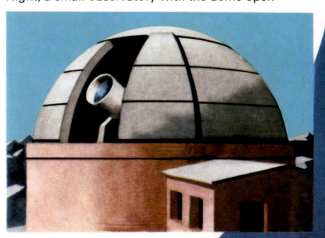

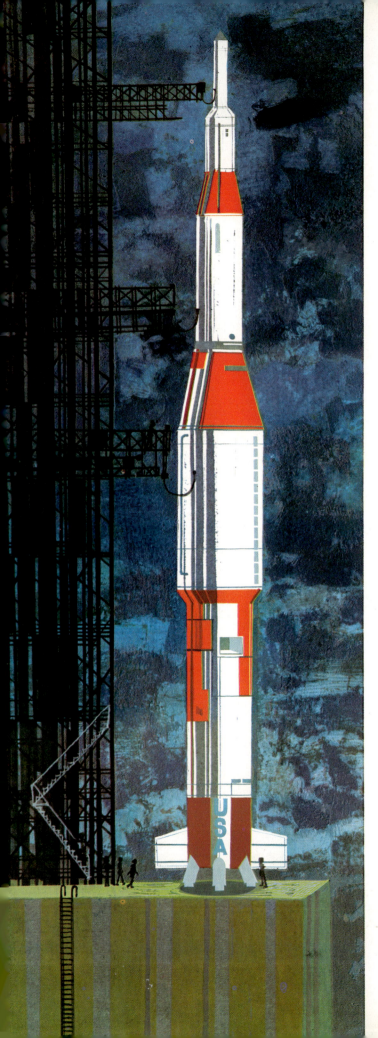

SPACE FLIGHT

A hundred years ago the Frenchman Jules Verne wrote the first science-fiction stories. In one of his books he describes a visit to the moon. Two men are projected into space inside a capsule which is fired like a shell from a gigantic gunbarrel buried vertically in the earth. "It will never happen," people said. They enjoyed reading about these fantasies, but they did not believe they would ever come true.

But on July 20th 1969 Jules Verne's story *did* come true. The lunar module *Eagle* landed safely on the moon. A few hours later the American astronaut Neil Armstrong became the first man to set foot on the moon's surface. There are two powerful forces to be overcome before a spaceship can leave the earth's atmosphere and enter space: the resistance of the air which surrounds the earth and the pull of the earth's gravity. To beat gravity a tremendous starting speed is needed. At the same time the spaceship must not be over-heated by friction as it leaves and re-enters the atmosphere. Otherwise it will become white-hot and burn up in a few seconds. Scientists managed to solve these problems and in 1957 the Russians launched the first *Sputnik*. The space age had begun.

Many more *satellites* were launched. Dogs were sent into space and brought safely back to earth. In 1961 the Russians launched another craft into space, and this time it contained a man! Major Yuri Gagarin had become the first astronaut.

Soon astronauts left their spaceships and "walked" in space. In 1968 the American spaceship *Apollo 8* flew round the moon and back to earth; later the first moon landing was made. Unmanned spaceships have been sent to distant planets, and a satellite laboratory, *Skylab*, is orbiting the earth, visited by scientists who carry out experiments under "weightless" conditions.

Modern science-fiction stories tell how men may live on remote planets and visit distant stars. You don't believe them? Neither did the people who read Jules Verne's stories!

The American astronauts walked on the moon

Moon 3476 km diameter
(2,160 miles)

Distance 384,000 km
(238,860 miles)

Earth
12,757 km diameter
(7,927 miles)

The size of the moon and the earth compared, with their distance apart

MOONSCAPE

The moon is our nearest neighbour in the sky, and it can easily be studied with good telescopes. There have been maps of the moon's surface for many years. They only showed one side however, for we cannot see the other side. Nowadays we have photographs and maps of the other side, thanks to the American astronauts. These men brought rocks and dust back to earth for scientists to examine. They set up experiments to discover new facts about the moon. The moon has no air and, as far as we know, no water. The side towards the sun has a temperature higher than boiling water, the other is twice as cold as it is at our North Pole.

The spacecraft which landed on the moon

171

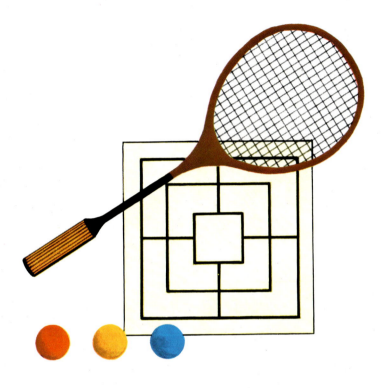

GAMES AND SPORTS

GAMES

At the top of this page you can see three children from three different parts of the world, a Red Indian boy, a girl from Japan and a little negro. They are playing ball, for such games are known all over the world and are believed to be the oldest kind of game.

There are some games which are peculiar to certain places. Cricket, for instance, is one of the national games of England. Sometimes a game is invented in a particular country and then becomes popular everywhere. This was the case with Dominoes, shown on the opposite page. The game was probably invented in Persia and is now played in most parts of the world. It is not only children who like playing games: most grown-ups also play games for pleasure and relaxation and we know that many famous people of the past enjoyed games. Henry VIII of England and Charles VI of France were tennis players, Drake liked bowls and a favourite game of the ancient Romans (grown-ups, not children) was Odd and Even, played with marbles.

Here you can see balls, toy bricks, ninepins, a peg top and a whipping top and coloured shapes from which patterns can be made. There are many other toys besides these, which you all know, toys such as

soldiers, marbles, bows and arrows, hoops and kites; and many of the things which are shown in this book can be toys: trains, cars and lorries, aeroplanes, bridges and ships.

Everyone knows how to play with toys like these. But there are other games which you play with other children and which have to be learnt. Among these are games like Rounders or board games such as Ludo and Snakes and Ladders. Some board games such as Chess, Draughts or Scrabble are more often played by bigger boys and girls and by grown-ups than by younger children.

They have to be played according to rules which are sometimes difficult to follow. The players have to think very hard. The game is like a battle between two armies, of which the two players are the generals.

The most skilful of all board games is Chess. Chess is a Persian word which means "king" and the game may have been invented in Persia although some people say it came from China. In any case it is a very ancient game. One of the earliest printed books is about Chess. The results of the game never depend on chance but on the skill of the players. Clever players sometimes keep a game of Chess going for a very long time, even as long as a year. The best players take a long time to think what to do next. So much interest is taken in Chess that international games are played just as with Tennis, Football and Cricket.

The game of Draughts is much simpler than Chess and the rules are not difficult. But no two games are ever alike so Draughts is never boring. You must always pay as much attention to the probable plans of your opponent as to your own. 'If he does that, I shall do this,', you must say to yourself.

Card games, like board games, are usually played by older boys and girls and grown-ups. Children very often like building houses of cards much better than playing games with them. And it is very difficult to build a house of cards and use up every single card. There are some card games, however, which are very easy to play. Among these are Snap, Old Maid and Rummy.

HOME MADE TOYS

You can always buy toys and games at the toy shop. But there are any number of toys you can make yourself. Very often you can use all kinds of things that nobody else wants and which would otherwise be thrown away. If there is anyone in the family who likes making things nothing must ever be thrown away without his permission.

It is surprising, for instance, what a lot of things can be made out of old cotton reels. The puppet playing ball on the left would not be nearly so nice without his head which is made out of half a cotton reel. His body is a cigarette packet covered with paper and his arms and legs have been cut out with a fretsaw. The balls are large wooden beads and he has a small bead for a neck. When you pull the strings the balls go up in the air. The puppet never fails to catch them again. Sometimes his head jerks up as well.

Bigger children like making model aeroplanes but it is a good idea to try making a kite before starting on aeroplanes. Making a kite is very good practice and will help you a great deal in aeroplane-building. To make a kite you need paper which is not too thick, yards and yards of string, a strip of lath to form the backbone of the kite and a piece

of split cane to make the cross-piece. The tail should be ten times as long as the kite itself. Kites were invented by the Chinese.

The picture at the bottom of this page shows you how to make a boat out of cardboard without using wood or a carpentry set. It is best to use stout, pliable card. Stick the joints with Sellotape, then cover the body of the boat with plastic paint. This will make it quite waterproof. If you want it to be a sailing boat you must give it a keel weighted with a nail. The mast is a twig, the sail is of thin paper.

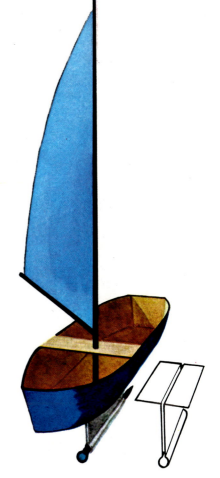

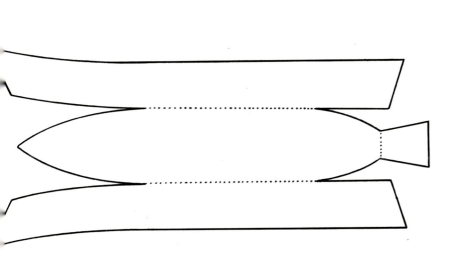

INDOOR EXERCISES OUTDOOR SPORTS

As far back as the time of the ancient Greeks and Romans people realised that exercise was good for their health. But there have been periods in history, such as the eighteenth century, when athletics were almost forgotten. Nowadays most children start doing gymnastic exercises at school and very often this is their favourite lesson. But outdoor sports are far more exciting. There are a number of athletic sports which can be enjoyed either alone or in competition with others. Some of these need special apparatus and others, like running, need none. In all cases it is necessary to persevere in order to improve. Everyone will agree that practice makes perfect.

The picture at the bottom of this page shows a gymnasium. On the left you can see ribstalls, poles and a rope. You can also see a horizontal bar, a horse, ladders and parallel bars on which someone is just doing a handstand.

The right-hand page shows a large sports ground and a stadium with a stand for spectators. Watching others is a favourite sport of those who do not play games themselves.

Car park

Stands

Football field and running track

Hall for gymnastics and table tennis

Tennis courts

Golf course

The sports ground is drawn
to scale: 1 inch = 80 feet

WATER SPORTS

If you can only swim like a brick you should never go sailing. You must first learn to swim like a fish, not only to sail but because swimming is one of the best of sports.

The picture shows a boating centre on a lake. On the left a water-skier is being drawn along by a motor boat. There is a small flat-bottomed sailing boat in front of the skier and to the right of it someone is paddling a canoe. Farther towards you is a collapsible canoe. The boat in the middle of the picture is a large cruising yacht in which quite long journeys can be made. The man in the sailing boat moored to the landing stage is busy taking down the sails. Close by is a boat anchored to a buoy. Its sails and deck are covered with a tarpaulin. On the right, on the mobile landing stage, a racing yacht has been hoisted up out of the water. You can tell by the large, heavy keel which prevents the yacht from capsizing in a strong beam or side wind that it is a very fast boat.

Right in the front of the picture you can see a racing skiff, a long, light, narrow boat with a sliding seat for one oarsman using short oars known as sculls. Yachtsmen speak a language of their own. They talk about "luffing", which means to steer nearer to the direction of the wind; "left" and "right" become "port" and "starboard"; the front ("fore") end of a boat they call the bow, and the back ("aft" or "after") is the stern. If you can talk the language you are half way to being a sailor!

WINTER SPORTS

It is winter. The bright sun cannot melt the snow that lies thick on the mountains. It is time to go ski-ing. It is extraordinary to think that until about 100 years ago hardly anybody had heard of ski-ing. The Scandinavians were the only people who knew how to ski at that time and the word "ski" is a Norwegian word.

The village people in other mountainous countries learned how to ski from the towns-folk who had watched the Swedes and the Norwegians doing it. But that was 100 years ago. Now every child who is lucky enough to live in the mountains spends the whole winter on skis and in the holidays he is joined by other children from countries where there is no snow.

This is the last big picture in our book and it shows a winter sports hotel, a mountain railway to bring the guests up from the valley down below and a ski lift, invented by a lazy-bones who hated climbing and only wanted to glide down the slopes.

CALENDAR

I

JANUARY
31 days

The New Year opens with parties and good wishes. The fifth is Twelfth Night, after which our Christmas decorations must be taken down. Country people used to think that if they were left till Candlemas, February 2nd, bad luck would follow. The sixth is the feast of the Three Wise Men, who came from the East to the Stable in Bethlehem.

II

FEBRUARY
28 days

In some parts of Europe the days before Lent are given up to masquerading. On Shrove Tuesday, the last day before Lent, it is the custom to eat pancakes. Every fourth year February has an extra day and we call this Leap Year. It comes about because the earth takes a few hours longer than 365 days to go round the sun. In four years these hours add up to one day.

V

MAY
31 days

May is the "merry month" when summer seems already to have come. The hedges are white with hawthorn blossom and the fields are full of buttercups. The sun stands high and in some places cherries are ripe and asparagus is ready to eat. But the first thunderstorms of the year are to be expected and there is sometimes a frost to kill the young plants in the garden.

VI

JUNE
30 days

This is the month of roses, and more flowers are out now than at any other time. On the 21st the sun reaches its highest position in the sky. Summer begins on this date and this is the longest day in the year. The hours of darkness are very short and in the far north the sun does not set at all. St. John's Day, the 24th, is celebrated as Midsummer Day.

IX

SEPTEMBER
30 days

The days are getting shorter and on the 21st or 22nd, as in March, night and day are of equal length. It is the beginning of autumn, blackberries are ripe and fruit is being picked in the orchards. The birds of passage are getting ready for their long flight to the warm south. Many of them fly for thousands of miles. The swallow flies all the way to South Africa.

X

OCTOBER
31 days

The leaves are turning red, blustering winds blow, boys fly their kites and the last wild flower of the year, the autumn crocus, withers away. Vine growers still hope for a few days' sun to ripen the grapes, for a warm October means good wine. If hips and haws are plentiful it is said that a hard winter is on the way. The 31st is Hallowe'en.

III
MARCH
31 days

The winter is drawing to a close, the days are getting longer and longer and on the 20th or 21st there are exactly twelve hours between the rising and setting of the sun. This is the first day of spring. Violets and primroses and the furry willow catkins are out and the first swallows have arrived. There may still be snow, but the sun begins to feel warmer.

IV
APRIL
30 days

April 1st is All Fools' Day. It is better not to say anything about it beforehand if you want to make a fool of someone. Easter usually falls in April, though it can come at the end of March. Easter Sunday is always the first Sunday after the first full moon of spring. The daisies dot the grass, the bees are already busy and the cuckoo is heard.

VII
JULY
31 days

The hottest days of the year, the so-called dog days, fall in this month. They take their name from the dog star or Sirius, which at this time of year rises with the sun. But this brilliant star is only visible in the night sky during the autumn. The summer holidays begin in July. Towards the end of the month the days begin to get shorter.

VIII
AUGUST
31 days

The summer is slowly coming to an end. The corn has ripened and the farmers are working in the fields with their great reaping machines. Heather and herbs such as thyme, camomile, arnica and valerian thrive in the heat. Sunflowers sometimes grow taller than a man. The seeds from these great flowers are stored as food for birds during the winter.

XI
NOVEMBER
30 days

The nights are long and cold and during the short day the sun is often hidden by fog and clouds. November 1st is All Saints' Day and the 5th is Guy Fawkes'. The cry of the tawny owl is frequently heard at night. The trees are quite bare and it may snow before the month is over. It is now time to be buying our Christmas presents.

XII
DECEMBER
31 days

December 6th is the day of St. Nicholas, the patron saint of children. Winter begins on the 21st, the shortest day of the year. On the 24th, Christmas Eve, the lights on the Christmas tree are lit and carols are sung. On the last night of the year we gather together to celebrate the coming year and when the hour of midnight strikes we all wish each other a happy New Year.

INDEX

WARD LOCK'S
FIRST PICTURE ENCYCLOPEDIA

in colour

Written and illustrated by Herbert Pothorn

With more than a thousand coloured pictures